'Where's Harry?'

£1

'Where's Harry?'

My Story by

HARRY CARPENTER

PELHAM BOOKS

PELHAM BOOKS

Published by the Penguin Group
27 Wrights Lane, London W8 5TZ
Viking Penguin Inc., 375 Hudson Street, New York, New York 10014, USA
Penguin Books Australia Ltd, Ringwood, Victoria, Australia
Penguin Books Canada Ltd, 10 Alcorn Avenue, Toronto, Ontario, Canada M4V 3B2
Penguin Books (NZ) Ltd, 182–190 Wairau Road, Auckland 10, New Zealand

Penguin Books Ltd, Registered Offices: Harmondsworth, Middlesex, England

First published in Great Britain in September 1992
Copyright © Harry Carpenter 1992

Typeset in Linotron Century Old Style, 11 on 13pt.

Printed and bound in Great Britain by
Butler & Tanner Ltd, Frome and London

A CIP catalogue record for this book is available from the British Library.

ISBN 0 7207 2013 3

To Peter Dimmock, who gave me the big chance

Photographic Acknowledgements

The author and publishers are grateful to the following for permission to reproduce copyright photographs: Allsport, 97, 102, 142, 143, 145 (bottom), 162, 164, 165, 166, 167; BBC, 48 (bottom), 54, 68 (bottom), 119, 120, 127, 147; *Boxing News*, 30, 31, 33, 45, 57, 58, 63, 125, 129, 130; Harry Carpenter, 76, 88, 90, 124; *Daily Mail*, 47; Francis-Thompson Studios, 68 (top); Greyhound Racing Association, 96; Hulton Deutsch Collection, 13, 21, 23, 26, 28, 32, 37, 38, 51, 64, 65, 77, 78, 86, 106, 114, 116 (left), 133, 134, 136, 155, 160; Ken Lewis, 94; Richard McLaren, Scope Features, 149; Matthews' News and Photo Agency, 25; Mike Pearce, 99; The Press Association, 44, 55, 71, 75, 128, 139, 140, 141, 159; Rex Features/Jon Lyons, 95; D. Rowe, 27, 48 (top), 158; S & G Press Agency, 61, 79, 80, 82, 101, 105, 109, 110, 111, 112, 113, 115, 116 (right), 117, 118, 121, 132, 145 (top), 146, 151 (top), 153, 154, 157. Every effort has been made to trace the copyright owners, but if there have been any omissions in this respect we apologise and will be pleased to make appropriate acknowledgement in any further editions.

Contents

1	You Have to Start Somewhere	9
2	The Most Significant Victory	20
3	'Feeding a Bowl of Blood to a Tiger'	40
4	'Get Out There and Fight'	53
5	Sprinting Through Mexico City	67
6	'Float Like a Butterfly, Sting Like a Bee'	74
7	A New Set of Friends	93
8	Dead Men's Shoes	108
9	The Triumvirate	123
10	The Time Had Come to Relax a Bit	144
11	'Know What I Mean, Harry?'	163
	Index	173

This led to twenty-five Open Championships. If only I'd been good enough to play in them . . .

1

You Have to Start Somewhere

The letter that shaped my life dropped on the mat at home one day in 1948. I had never heard of Michael Henderson, but he was obviously important: he signed himself Television Outside Broadcasts Producer. He wanted me to go along and see him. I was twenty-two years old.

Only a callow youth pushing his luck would have written to the BBC in the first place. I was offering myself as a boxing commentator. Not to BBC Radio, mind you. I knew where to draw the line. Radio was big time. They had stars like Stewart MacPherson, Raymond Glendenning and W. Barrington Dalby. Kid Carpenter had no chance of mixing with the heavyweights. But television . . . well, there was no harm in trying.

We had a TV at home, a nine-inch screen, black and white. It was part of a massive, walnut-faced radiogram-cum-television set. You lifted a lid to reveal the wireless and the gramophone.

Ah, the gramophone . . . 78rpm, brittle shellac ten- or twelve-inch records, which you piled up eight at a time on the spindle and they clattered on to the turntable to be played by a steel needle. Or, if you were very fussy about your records, by a thorn, which had to be sharpened back to a point after every playing . . .

To watch the television, you slid back a metal grille on the front of the set and, hey presto, there was the screen. Nobody else I knew had a television in 1948. There were only 12,000 sets in the whole of

the country and if you didn't live within twenty-five miles of the transmitter at Alexandra Palace, you couldn't get the programmes anyway.

But in our semi-detached at Shirley, near Croydon, my family was already on nodding terms with Mary Malcolm, Sylvia Peters and Macdonald Hobley. They were the presentation announcers, sleekly encased in evening clothes, who smiled so sweetly and said: 'Now it's time for amateur boxing . . .'

Michael Henderson turned out to be only a year or two older than I was – and I *had* heard of him. He was the same Michael Henderson who was doing Boat Race and Rugby Union commentaries. That will give you some idea of how small a concern TV was in those days: producers doubled up as commentators. Henderson's office was at 35, Marylebone High Street, London, W1, then the administration headquarters of BBC Television Outside Broadcasts, an address later taken over by *Radio Times*. Henderson was shock-haired and studious; he beamed through spectacles as he softly questioned me on what I knew of boxing. I had to admit I was low on practical experience, but fair on theory.

Had he, I asked, heard of Henry Carpenter of Peckham, who was that year's ABA flyweight champion and was going to box for Britain in the Olympic Games at Wembley? Henry was a distant cousin. I hoped, naïvely, to ride along on Henry's reputation. The beaming stopped and Michael dropped the bombshell: 'Would you care to take an audition *now*?'

Panic bubbled. Now? What does he mean, now? How can I audition as a boxing commentator sitting one floor up in an office in London's West End? 'If you agree,' he was saying, 'we'll go into the room next door. I've got a film projector in there. I'll show you some film, you can commentate over it, and we'll record it.'

Having come this far, there was no point in refusing. This would be the one and only chance. I swallowed hard and said OK. 'Oh, there's just one thing,' said Michael. 'I'm afraid I don't have any boxing film, but I do have a bit of football and I can show you that.'

Football? I didn't want to be a football commentator. Why did I ever send off that letter? But soon we were next door, blinds drawn, screen up, projector switched on. Michael sat me at a table with a microphone and a tape recorder. He shoved a piece of paper in front of me. It was headed 'Fulham *v* Everton, Craven Cottage'. There was a description of what had happened so far, the half-time score, the names of the players.

Top left *With my mother, Adelaide, at Cliftonville, Kent. She was about thirty years old; I was five and a natty dresser. Who sports a tie on the beach today?*

Top right *Ashburton School, Croydon,* circa *1930. That's me with my socks dangling. Why couldn't I have a seat like the rest of them?*

Bottom left *Jolly Jack Carpenter, 1943, having just enrolled in the Royal Navy and already flouting the rules. The cap is supposed to be worn dead straight.*

Bottom right *Mum and Dad in middle age, living it up at the Fish Trade's Ball at London's Grosvenor House.*

Michael said, 'Just spend five minutes mugging up what you can, then we'll go ahead.' And we did. The camera must have been on the Craven Cottage roof; the players were merely ants scurrying hither and thither. For ten or fifteen minutes, I burbled whatever came into my mind. I cannot tell you if it made sense – probably not. Then, mercifully, the film was stopped, Michael thanked me and escorted me to the door. 'We'll have a listen to it and let you know what we think,' he said. I tottered out into Marylebone High Street and knew for certain that I would never, ever be a boxing commentator.

It had been an impertinent move, anyway. I was just a budding journalist on the fringes of sport. I had never reported boxing. Most of what I knew about it came from my father. He was in fish. Harry Carpenter senior ran a wholesale business in Billingsgate Market alongside the Thames at London Bridge. A lot of good fighters came out of the market.

Jack Solomons, Britain's leading fight promoter for twenty years after World War II, was a fishmonger. He bought fish from my father. Dad loved boxing. Before the war I was allowed to stay up and listen to the big fights on the wireless: Len Harvey, Jack Petersen, Larry Gains, Jack Doyle, Jock McAvoy, Eric Boon, Arthur Danahar . . . These were household names; at least, they were in the house where I lived.

To this day I can conjure up the booming, magisterial tones of Howard Marshall describing those fights in the 1930s. Just as clearly, I can recall the Canadian twang of Bob Bowman coming through our wireless in the small hours of August 1937. I had been shaken awake and came downstairs at three o'clock in the morning, in pyjamas and dressing-gown, to hear Bowman's graphic blow-by-blow commentary, live from New York, on Tommy Farr's bid to take the world heavyweight championship from Joe Louis. I was eleven years old.

Perhaps these were the moments when the idea was born that I, too, might one day report a big fight. If so, I kept it to myself. It never occurred to me that the day would come when I would be able to count Louis and Farr among my friends.

There are rewards in my present job which transcend even the highly satisfying pursuits of fronting and commentating. I can never forget the joy of working alongside Tommy Farr at the ringside and travelling to fights with him. He wrote about boxing for the *Sunday Pictorial*.

Was this really the man I got up at 3 am for in 1937, who defied the immortal Joe Louis for fifteen rounds? I could seldom get a serious word from him about that fight. I expect he was fed up with people

In 1958 Harringay arena shut down. With Jack Solomons were champions Max Baer, Len Harvey, Jack Petersen, Bruce Woodcock, Randolph Turpin, Don Cockell, Eric Boon, Rinty Monaghan, Terry Downes, Henry Armstrong, Gus Lesnevich, Sammy McCarthy, Peter Waterman and Johnny Williams.

mentioning it. All he ever said in his lilting Welsh accent was: 'I only have to hear the name Joe Louis and my nose bleeds.'

I certainly did not contemplate my future friendships with these two men in 1948. What first-hand knowledge of boxing I had was strictly on the amateur side of the sport. Dad was a vice-president of the Penge and Beckenham Amateur Boxing Club and we went to the occasional show together. The club coach was a wee, wise man called Dan Titchener who later looked after England's national squad.

Cockney Dan was a kindly soul blessed with infinite patience who listened to my damn-fool questions about the techniques of boxing and gave me expert answers. Whatever I may know today about that side of the sport is based entirely on what Dan Titchener taught me. I don't come across too many boxing coaches today, amateur or pro, who have half his knowledge. If old Dan is gazing down from the Paradise gym and listening in, I just want to say God bless you, sir, and thank you.

When I went to see Michael Henderson, I was working on a magazine called *Speedway Gazette*, as assistant editor, if you please. I fitted in between Basil Storey, the editor, and Reg, the office boy. We had one other staff member: our roving photographer, John Alexander. Now there was a character.

John wore heavy spectacles, had lank, Brylcreemed hair, a three-day growth of beard, and clothes that had seen better days. None of this apparently deterred a regiment of young ladies who were only too keen to take their clothes off in front of his lens. Occasionally he would drop in at the office and sling down the latest nude pin-up picture in front of me. I didn't mind, but one day dear old Vic Woodcock, the head printer, a man of Victorian respectability, happened to see one of John's masterpieces and was offended. He wagged a reproving finger in John's face and spluttered, 'Suppose this girl were your sister?' John replied, 'She *is* my sister.'

Between us we put sixteen pages together every week and they were printed at Argus Press, between Fleet Street and the Embankment. Basil Storey was a tight-lipped, chain-smoking dynamo from Whitley Bay, a sports reporter of the old school, who hero-worshipped Newcastle United and Jackie Milburn.

He did most of the writing, while I made up the pages and put the paper to bed. These were the post-war boom days of speedway when the world championship final drew close on 100,000 fans to Wembley Stadium. They came bedecked in rosettes and long scarves in team colours, and were armed with giant rattles which when whirled gave out a raucous, rasping sound. It was the only way they could be sure of making themselves heard above the raucous, rasping sound of the souped-up bikes. Speedway supporters had – presumably still have – fierce loyalty to their teams and favourite riders. The mighty ones of that era were the brothers Jack and Norman Parker, Vic Duggan, Tommy Price, Eric Chitty, Alec Statham and Graham Warren.

Truth to tell, I was very much a stand-off observer of the sport and for that I blamed Jack Parker, the leading rider of his time. I had first seen speedway racing at Crystal Palace when I was seven or eight years old. They raced on black cinders in those pioneering days. The riders stuck a leg out behind them and wrestled their slithering bikes

Right *They don't write 'em like this any more . . . a little number I ran up in my early Fleet Street days. The price? Just 12½p in today's money.*

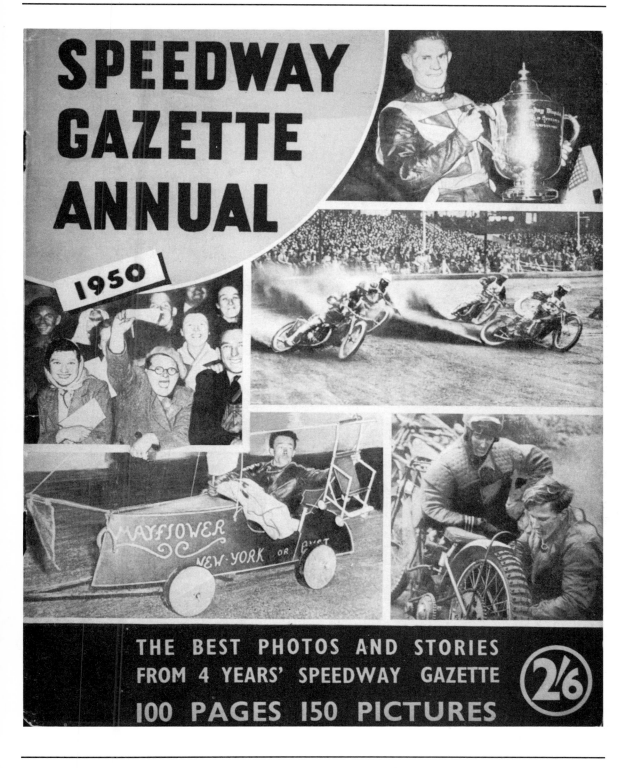

round the bends as best they could. It was called leg-trailing and it was the accepted style.

They roared round the track in huge arcs, sending up vast plumes of flying cinders. I loved it. But after the war, Jack Parker discovered that by sticking your left leg out *in front*, the bike could be made to hug the bends and that, after all, was the shorter way round. When I was on the *Speedway Gazette* just about every star rode that way. Very clever, but rather unexciting, I thought. What's more, they had done away with those lovely, dirty old cinders and replaced them with clean, boring red shale. I had only one hero left. His name was Oliver Hart and I respected him because he still raced the old-fashioned way. He was known as 'The Last of the Leg Trailers'. Sadly, he didn't seem to win very often.

Basil Storey will be remembered by old-time *Daily Express* readers: he contributed ice hockey and speedway reports for years. He learned his craft in the north-east of England and could turn his hand to almost any form of writing, but would have loved to earn his living writing boys' fiction. He was an admirer of Frank Richards (alias Charles Hamilton), the creator of Billy Bunter, who spent a lifetime churning out the Greyfriars and St Jim's School stories for the *Magnet* and the *Gem*.

During our time together on the *Speedway Gazette*, Basil and I produced a short-lived magazine called *Boys' World* (every other Thursday, threepence). We declared ourselves in ringing tones on the front cover: 'For Boys Who Will Make the Man's World of Tomorrow'. The paper contained five or six stories. I wrote one of them: Cliff Crane, Film Stuntman. Don't ask me how he found the time, but Basil wrote four stories every fortnight, and the remaining one, Atom Boy, about a young robot who sorted out the villains, was contributed by Clem Macartney, a mate of Basil's who worked as publicity man for Wembley Stadium. *Boys' World* lasted about a year. I have never met anyone who read it.

On Saturday afternoons I took a train from East Croydon to Charing Cross, hopped aboard a tram on the Embankment, rode up through the tunnel under Kingsway, and came out at Gray's Inn Road, the home of Kemsley House, one of the giant fortresses of the newspaper world at that time. I had got myself a weekly stipend, a guinea (£1.05) or two, on the *Sunday Graphic*, sub-editing on the Sports Desk.

Bob Read, a bumbling, amiable bear of a man, was Sports Editor. His assistant was a shrewd, sharp-faced character called Bill Gibbons, who spoke in clipped, correct English. If you told him

The short-lived magazine in which I tried – and failed – to become a world famous author of boys' fiction.

something he couldn't quite believe, his lips would purse and he would utter just two words: 'Surely not?' I found this so compelling I still use it as an idiom today. Bill would toss a soccer reporter's phoned-in copy down on the table, and tell you how much space he had for it; it was your job to turn the execrable English into something the *Sunday Graphic* reader would be dying to read. Unhappily, it was the *Sunday Graphic* that was dying and eventually I shot off to the *People*, where I found myself working alongside a young chap called Paul Fox, who wrote the soccer highlights column. I didn't realise how he would figure in my life later on.

You can see what a confounded cheek it was for this upstart from the lower echelons of Fleet Street to offer himself to the august BBC and I reckoned my afternoon of humiliation in the offices of Mike Henderson had been well deserved. Months passed and I continued to put the *Speedway Gazette* to bed, got Cliff Crane involved in ever more footling adventures, listened to the exploits of Bruce Woodcock and Freddie Mills on the wireless and forgot entirely the foolish notion of getting myself into television.

. . . Until the phone rang at home one Tuesday night in January 1949, and a voice said: 'You won't know me, but my name is Peter Dimmock and I'm producing some amateur boxing for BBC Television on Saturday night. I'm afraid my usual commentator has gone off abroad somewhere and I'm stuck. Could you stand in for him?'

I said of course, but it would be a lie to say I was thrilled; terror-stricken, yes. The next four days gave me a passable idea of what the condemned man must go through. I had never broadcast and never written a single word about boxing. But, come Saturday, they would sit me down at ringside, shove a microphone into my hand, and I would reveal to the TV audience my authoritative knowledge of the sport.

On the Thursday a letter arrived from Michael Henderson: 'Dear Mr Carpenter, I am very glad that you are willing to have a try at the boxing on Saturday, 15 January . . . I would point out that you must collect all the information about the boxers before Saturday. You will remember that our present policy on boxing commentary for television is to say only what is absolutely necessary during the rounds and then to comment and observe on the course of the bout during the interval.'

I was utterly, thoroughly frightened and wished, once again, that I hadn't written that damned letter in the first place. I persuaded Dad to phone Dan Titchener, the boxing coach, to ask if he'd give me a few hints on how to tackle a commentary. I went round to the Penge and Beckenham gym and Dan did his best to help. He never once, in later years, claimed any credit. Neither did he ever mention what must have been patently obvious to him at the time: that I was too inexperienced to do the job.

In today's highly sophisticated world of television, an audience of a million is small beer. How, then, do you rate a live, amateur boxing transmission of fifty minutes which went out on a Saturday night at half-past nine (what they now call prime-time) and was watched by no more than 50,000 viewers, all of them living in the London area? But that is how it was. If it hadn't been so small, so insignificant, a novice like myself would not have survived.

Peter Dimmock, a BBC producer, ex-racing reporter, currently doubling up as a commentator on ice-hockey matches, was televising a very ordinary amateur club show from the Rotax factory canteen in Willesden, in the north London suburbs. I made my reluctant way there on the Saturday afternoon by bus and tube. I was years away from owning a car.

When I arrived I discovered I was not the sole commentator. Leo Hoban, an Eton games master, had been called in to supply the inter-round summaries. He, too, was broadcasting for the first time. The pair of us were told that you had to wear headphones and through these you would not only hear Mr Dimmock directing *you*, but his comments to cameramen would also be available while you were trying to put some words together.

Peter, to put it mildly, had a vigorous way of directing, and my principal memory of that dreadful evening is a torrent of abuse coming through the headphones, not all of it for Leo and Harry, but certainly some of it. Poor Peter. What had he done to deserve two tyro commentators at once? Shamefully, I remember almost nothing of the actual boxing, except that one of the participants was a boy called Allan Buxton, a lightweight and a member of that illustrious Watford boxing family which included brother Alex, a famous professional fighter.

What on earth *did* I say that night in January 1949? Fortunately, we'll never know. Video recording had not been invented. It would not come along for another ten years or so. Posterity has been spared those awful, faltering comments from the factory canteen in Willesden. But you have to start somewhere.

It seemed to me, as I got back into the tube, depressed and still trembling from the nightmare of it all, that I had not only made a start in television, I had come to a dead stop as well.

2

The Most Significant Victory

For two months I believed my career in television was over. I received not a word from the BBC, until finally, in March, a letter came. Somebody up there at Marylebone High Street liked me and his name was Michael Henderson: 'I can now say that we hope you will be interested to make further trials and training at Outside Broadcasts, when time allows and the site is suitable.' With some eagerness, I waited for the trials and the training. They never came. They still haven't. Instead, nine months after the Willesden debacle, they pitched me in at the deep end again at Lewisham Town Hall, another amateur boxing evening, this one organised by Downham Goldsmiths ABC.

I had a different producer, a genial, placid, pipe-smoking chap, Barrie Edgar, who called everyone 'cock' and nursed me through the evening with tender, loving care. There was even a 'G. Carpenter' on the bill (no relation) and the prizes were presented by none other than Mr Ron Johnson, captain of the New Cross speedway team. I felt I was among friends.

Among those boxing was Don Scott, who had won the Olympic light-heavyweight silver at Wembley the year before, and Terry Ratcliffe, of Bristol, one of the hardest hitters of the day, who a few months later would win the ABA welterweight title. Another competitor was Freddie King, from the Robert Browning Club in South London, whom I still meet today when he works in the corner of many a famous pro.

A budding boxing writer on the Sporting Record, *1954. The window overlooked Fleet Street and the typewriter is now in the Victoria and Albert Museum.*

I suspect I didn't do too badly on this occasion, although I still would not want to hear any of it played back. I also had a smoothly confident inter-round summariser, Tony van den Bergh, a bearded wit who won fame later as a TV and radio documentary writer and producer.

From this evening in Lewisham sprang increasingly frequent commentary jobs on TV, but always *amateur* boxing. The professional side of the sport at this time was almost totally banned from the screen at the edict of the British Boxing Board of Control, who saw what had happened in the USA, where TV screens were awash with pro boxing. The inevitable result was that only the most important fights in America attracted any sort of paying crowd.

As 1950 began, my personal and working lives were transformed. I was offered a sub-editor's job at £12 a week by the weekly *Sporting Record*, an all-sports paper printed, like the *Speedway Gazette*, at Argus Press and owned by Brigadier Michael Wardell, a tough Canadian who had lost an eye in the war. He had a way of dropping in at the office when least expected and barking out fierce criticism of the paper. With his black eyepatch he cut a piratical figure and behind his back he was known as 'the Grand Military Handicap'.

We worked at 184, Fleet Street, flanked by the Kardomah Café and a Methodist chapel. One floor above were the offices of our sister paper, the monthly *World Sports*. An eager young assistant up there was a chap named Brian Moore. I believe he became a football commentator. Across the road and down an alley was The Clachan, where I learned to drink beer under the baleful eye of Mrs Rothwell, the fiercest publican in London.

The *Sporting Record* had top-line contributors: Kay Stammers (tennis), Victor Barna (table tennis), Pat Besford (swimming), Ivan Sharpe (football), Geoffrey Gilbey (racing) and Neville Cardus (cricket). The Cardus copy was delivered by courier from the National Liberal Club in Whitehall Place, where it was written in spidery longhand on foolscap sheets. The first time it landed on my desk I felt as if I had been entrusted with sacred scrolls. I never altered a word. Breaking it up into paragraphs and putting a headline on it seemed daring enough.

The boxing column was written by Lainson Wood of the *Daily Telegraph* under an assumed name. Lainson was a huge man of considerable talent who could write just as comfortably about real tennis or rackets as he could about the seamy side of boxing. His enormous bulk and his propensity for falling gently asleep and snoring at the ringside afforded a lot of amusement, but his report on a big fight was as accurate and shrewd as you would find anywhere.

God bless him, Lainson changed my life. His weekly piece for the *Sporting Record* was probably an additional burden he didn't much relish. Whatever the reason, his copy turned up perilously late three weeks in a row. One morning, three months after I'd arrived at the *Record*, Bill Mann, the editor, a brusque wee Scot who sat opposite me by the big window overlooking Fleet Street, leant across the desk and said: 'You've done a bit of boxing commentary on the television, haven't you?' I admitted I'd done a little. 'Good,' said Bill. 'I've fired Lainson. You're our new boxing writer.' Just like that.

In the coming years I worked alongside Lainson at the ringside around the world. He knew how I'd come by my job. He never spoke about it and he was never anything but friendly. I had a lot of respect for the fat man from the *Telegraph*.

A few weeks later, I married Phyl Matthews, a lovely young thing who was private secretary to Philip Dosse, the publisher of *Speedway Gazette*. She worked in an office above the Black and White milk bar on the corner of Bouverie Street and I turned up there one day clutching two free tickets for the Playhouse Theatre. That was how we started going out. Would it have happened but for those free tickets? I still ask her that today. She has her own back, though. She tells me she only accepted because she liked the look of my overcoat.

In September 1950, we spent our wedding night at Oddenino's Hotel in Regent Street and the following morning flew out of Northolt for the honeymoon in Paris. Then we took up residence in a tiny, top-floor furnished flat (shared bathroom: sixpence in the meter) over a sweetshop on Rosslyn Hill, Hampstead. We went to work by trolleybus and spent our Sunday evenings watching silent film classics at the Everyman Cinema. It was blissful.

There was a letter from Barrie Edgar waiting at Rosslyn Hill: 'Many congratulations. I rang the office to speak to you yesterday and they told me you were gaily (sic) honeymooning in Paris. We are hoping to televise the England-Ireland amateur boxing from Wembley on Friday 27 October and if you are free I would like you to do the inter-round commentaries.' The blow-by-blow commentator, he wrote, would be a new chap who had just come across from Ireland where he'd done a bit of boxing.

The new chap was Eamonn Andrews.

Eamonn Andrews v Sidney the Boxing Kangaroo. It was a publicity stunt for Paul Gallico's book Matilda. *I just wondered if the kangaroo understood what he was taking on. Eamonn was once Irish amateur middleweight champion.*

Eamonn and I worked regularly together on televised boxing. He did the blow-by-blow, I filled in between rounds. Eamonn had come across from Ireland to replace Stewart MacPherson as the host of radio's *Ignorance is Bliss*, a zany quiz show with Harold Berens and Gladys Hay.

Eamonn had been amateur middleweight champion of Ireland, so his knowledge of boxing was gained firsthand. My job was to fill in the background of the largely unknown amateurs we were dealing with. My journalistic training taught me to be inquisitive, so I beavered away in the dressing-room beforehand, asking boxers what their Christian names were (amateurs in those days appeared in the programme with initials only, as they sometimes still do today), what they did for a living, whether they were married and what their hobbies were.

This sort of information had never been offered in commentaries before. It fleshed out the characters on the screen and made them into real people, rather than two-dimensional figures. Well, that's my story, and *Punch* came out with a cartoon to back me up. A husband and wife are sitting in their armchairs watching boxing on TV. One of the boxers is laid out flat on his back. Mum is saying to Dad: 'That's a terrible thing to do to a twenty-four-year-old unemployed plumber with three children who plays the guitar for a hobby.'

Writing 1,500 words a week on boxing has to be one of life's cushy numbers. I wrote the piece on Friday, did my Saturday stint at the *People*, took Sunday off and still had four days to kill. There was no better place to do it than Jack Solomons' gym. I spent most of my waking hours there for the next four years.

During those early years of the 1950s Solomons' gym was the focal point of British boxing. Solomons was Mr Boxing. Ostensibly, the ruler was the British Boxing Board of Control, but the man with the grip on the purse-strings was Solomons. He had access to the main arenas in London and he worked closely with provincial promoters like Reg King in Nottingham, Joe Jacobs in Leicester and Johnny Best in Liverpool.

Fight managers knew that if they didn't play ball with Solomons or his promotional chums, their fighters would be out of work most of the time. It sounds vicious and it might engage the interest of the Monopolies Commission today, but that is how it was. Solomons' rule lasted from 1946 into the 1960s.

Arguably that period was one of the brightest and best in British boxing's history. Jack Solomons was a brilliant showman. A big

I spent a lot of time having my ear bent by Jack Solomons, the shrewdest promoter Britain has ever had. Canadian heavyweight Larry Gains (centre) boxed before my time. He beat the giant Primo Carnera, went in with Len Harvey and Jack Petersen, and was the first black boxer to win an Empire title.

Derby-eve fight night out of doors at the White City called for ringside evening dress and women smothered in fur and diamonds. In case the customers got bored waiting for the boxing to start, Joe Loss and his Band entertained them from the ring.

The trumpet fanfare heralding the arrival of the warriors for the main event is old hat today. Solomons introduced it. He had an agreement with Frank Gentle, boss of the Greyhound Racing Association, for the use of Harringay and the White City. It was GRA policy to greet the arrival of greyhounds on the track with a florid ceremonial fanfare. Jack heard it, borrowed it, and played it. You hear the same fanfare at boxing shows today.

Solomons was once a fishmonger with a shop in Ridley Road in London's East End. In the early 1930s he opened a Sunday fight club in Devonshire Road, Hackney. He called it the Devonshire Club. Customers could have a late breakfast while they watched the boxing. Solomons was no fool. He took their money at the door, then sold them his own kippers.

Jack's rise to supremacy in British boxing began with a fighter called Eric Boon. Sixteen years old, he cycled to London from Chatteris in Cambridgeshire, fought six two-minute rounds for 30 bob (£1.50), then cycled all the way home.

Eric Boon (right) *was the keystone to Jack Solomons' success as a promoter. Despite the shut eye, he'd just beaten Arthur Danahar in their famous 1939 fight.*

'Boy' Boon, as he soon became known, was a tearaway lightweight with a damaging punch. Solomons became his manager. Within four years Boon knocked out the respected Dave Crowley to become British champion and in 1939 defended his title against Arthur Danahar, a skilful but light-hitting former ABA champion.

Their fight was the sensation of its time and more than half a century later people still talk about it. The demand for tickets was so great that for the first time anywhere in the world a cinema offered closed-circuit television to accommodate an overflow crowd. Boon's harder punching overcame the courage of Danahar, and the referee, W. Barrington Dalby, stopped the fight in the fourteenth round.

Boon's success swept Solomons to national prominence and when post-war boxing got under way, Jack was the country's top promoter. His gym was just a short walk from Piccadilly Circus, at 41, Great Windmill Street, opposite the Windmill Theatre. This home of nude revues had remained open throughout the war and its slogan was 'We Never Clothed'. The Windmill opened its doors at midday, and each morning as I walked up the street the queue of men in shabby raincoats was already forming.

Across the road, the gym – and Solomons' office – was on the second floor. A seedy billiard hall occupied the first. You trod gingerly past the smelly dustbins on the landing, walked up one more flight and entered the gym past a box-office window where Bobby Broadribb sold the fight tickets. Above the hatch a printed notice warned: 'No Complimentaries'. This was the real, hard world of the fight game.

Jack's office was half taken up by a big leather-topped desk littered with record books, fight contracts and a phone. The walls were smothered in old photos, mostly of Jack with his famous friends. There was a drinks cupboard, permanently open. To get to Jack you had to get past the outer office and Jack's girl Friday, the efficient and overworked Terry Donner, who guarded the guv'nor with built-in radar that could spot a chiseller a mile away.

For a time I was chairman of the Boxing Writers' Club, which is how I came to be handing a present to the lively and lovely Terry Donner. She was personal assistant to Jack Solomons and knew more about insider-dealing in boxing than most people.

Promoter Solomons, no lightweight, like a babe in the arms of Ewart Potgieter, the tallest fighter I've seen. The South African, who came here in 1955, stood 7ft 2in, dwarfing Freddie Mills. Unfortunately, he couldn't fight and had nothing more than freak value.

The gym had a ring Jack brought with him from the old Devonshire Club. A heavy leather punchbag swung from the ceiling. Faded gold lettering proclaimed it a gift from America's Joe Vella and his fighter Gus Lesnevich, who had lost the world light-heavyweight title to Freddie Mills in one of Solomons' most glittering post-war shows.

Fighters who came to train were charged half-a-crown (12½p) a day, payable into the palm of Nat Seller, who ran the place for Solomons. Nat trained and 'managed' fighters for Jack, who under the Board rules of those days was not allowed to be both promoter and manager, although we all knew he was.

The gym was always busy . . . fighters working out, weigh-ins for shows, Pressmen in and out all the time, and managers using it to do their deals. It was the perfect place for a young boxing writer to learn the business. I made the most of it.

As the accredited correspondent of the *Sporting Record* I was now in a position to claim a working Press seat ringside and I went to as many shows as I could. I was lucky. This was the time Randolph Turpin was making his way to the top.

Turpin, in that heady year 1950–51, was the most exciting fighter I have ever seen. He was physically magnificent and his reputation as a knockout puncher destroyed his opponents' resolve long before they got in the ring with him. Mike Tyson had the same effect on men forty years later. Lainson Wood called Turpin's punch the 'lightning strike'.

In September 1950, at Watford's football ground, I watched Turpin destroy Eli Elandon from the Belgian Congo with one flashing left hook to the chin in the second round. The following month at Harringay he knocked out the skilful Albert Finch of Croydon in five rounds and became middleweight champion of Britain, a title his elder brother Dick had previously held.

There was the extraordinary night at Harringay in February 1951, when Turpin left-hooked Luc van Dam of Holland on the chin just thirty-five seconds into their fight. I swear van Dam was unconscious as he began to fall. Turpin was so quick, he smacked a right on the Dutchman's chin long before he hit the floor. Van Dam was spark out for ten minutes and Turpin had won the European title in forty-eight seconds.

That same night, Don Cockell, Britain's light-heavyweight champion, opened up against Lloyd Marshall, an experienced American. A left hook cracked against Marshall's jaw, a right hand followed. Marshall crumpled up on the ropes and sagged slowly to the floor. It was fifteen minutes before he was able to leave the ring. Cockell had

Randolph Turpin's commanding physique was based on intense body-building. Between 1950 and '51 he was unbeatable. I have not seen many fighters who could punch as hard. But his private life was a shambles.

won in thirty-five seconds. The two main fights were over in less than a minute and a half between them.

The crowd didn't complain; they were delirious with excitement. The next day Solomons said Turpin would fight Sugar Ray Robinson for the middleweight championship of the world in Britain later that year. Oh, yeah? Pull the other one, Jack. But he turned out to be right.

In July 1951, just as Solomons predicted, the legendary Sugar Ray Robinson came to London to fight Randolph Turpin; I use the adjective justifiably. Robinson was thirty and had been a professional boxer for more than a decade. From 1946 to 1950 he was welterweight (10st 7lb) champion of the world. No one could beat him, so he moved up to middleweight (11st 6lb). In 133 fights, only one man had *ever* beaten him: Jake La Motta, the Bull of the Bronx, and that was back in 1943. Robinson had since beaten La Motta four times and on the last occasion, only a few months before he came to England, had won the world title from him. It was this championship he was putting up against Turpin.

No fighter in living memory had caused such interest in this country as Robinson. No fighter would again until Muhammad Ali arrived twelve years later. It was hardly surprising: apart from his extraordinary record, Robinson was a super showman. He travelled the world in regal style. His entourage included his barber, masseur, chauffeur, personal golf pro and a dwarf who acted as court jester.

Sugar Ray trained in Windsor, at the Star and Garter near the Castle, and commuted to and from London in a vast, heliotrope Cadillac. He was sleek, handsome and, as we all knew, one helluva fighter. That is, until he climbed through the ropes at Earl's Court on the night of 10 July 1951. That night he was a pretty ordinary performer. He had been touring the Continent the previous few

Randolph Turpin from Leamington Spa (left) has just achieved the most astonishing win in British boxing history. He's beaten the legendary world champion Sugar Ray Robinson at Earl's Court, London, July 1951. Turpin never had another moment as good, sliding from triumph to suicide.

weeks and lurid stories were rife about his bedroom exploits. True or false, his form at Earl's Court was well below what I had expected to see.

To me the fight was hugely disappointing. Robinson was cut in the seventh round; Turpin chased him hard, but never put him down. But if I sensed an anti-climax, I was probably alone. The fight went the full fifteen rounds and the celebrations began long before the final bell. The lifting of Turpin's arm by Eugene Henderson was the cue for 18,000 joyous people to strike up 'For He's a Jolly Good Fellow'. Now *I* started to get emotional. It was, after all, the most significant victory any British boxer had achieved in the twentieth century – but still not a great fight. Turpin's explosive punching had been nullified. Sugar Ray had done nothing but be warily defensive. Who cared? Our man had won.

Patriotism ran riot. Within twenty-four hours BBC Radio came in for scathing criticism. Raymond Glendenning had described the fight and Barry Dalby summed up between rounds. Between them they

Robinson spent a lot of time getting out of the way of Turpin's punches, but didn't throw too many himself.

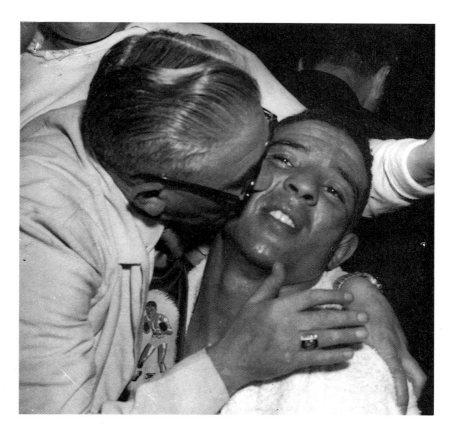

What a successful fighter has to suffer. Turpin, having outboxed Robinson, gets a kiss from his manager, George Middleton. Nothing in the fight was nearly as painful.

had given the impression that Robinson would surely come up with something exciting before the end (I had felt the same way) and at the end of the fourteenth round Barry said: 'If Turpin can stage a really grandstand finish in this final round, I think he may well snatch the verdict.'

There was nothing much wrong with that. But in the chauvinistic clamour of the moment, people felt that Turpin had been unfairly treated by these words. The papers made a lot of it and, incredibly, the BBC made Barry go on the air on the Saturday to explain himself. I felt – and still do – that he should have said: 'That's my opinion and I stick to it.' After all, he was a top class boxing referee. In his wisdom, Barry retracted the word 'snatch' and said he had meant to say 'clinch'. This unhappy incident convinced me that if I should receive similar criticism for an opinion, I would stand by it.

The last time I saw Sugar Ray Robinson, the supreme boxer of my time, we were in the BBC's New York offices. His days of wealth

One of my first radio commentaries, at Market Harborough in the early 1950s. Raymond Glendenning, with the handlebar moustache and the well-tailored suit, did the blow-by-blow stuff; I chipped in between rounds. Raymond was radio's top commentator at this time, handling half a dozen sports and royal occasions. He called me 'old boy', which puzzled me as I was quite a young boy.

were long over. He had made millions, but most of it went on bad business investments and an entourage that was too big and had been maintained for too long; and there were the beautiful women . . . and the bright lights.

He didn't stop boxing until 1965, when he was forty-four. Even when he was past his best, he kept on regaining the world middleweight title, four times in all. But in 1960, at the age of thirty-nine, he failed to get it back from Paul Pender in Pender's own city of Boston. In the run-up to the fight, I talked with Johnny Buckley, Pender's veteran, hard-bitten manager who had once handled Jack Sharkey, the world heavyweight champion. Buckley had no praise to spare for Robinson.

'The whole of boxing will be glad to see the back of him,' he snapped. I asked why. 'He's too greedy,' said Buckley. 'He wants all the dough. My fighter has to go in there for peanuts.'

It didn't take a genius to understand that with almost any opponent other than Robinson, Pender would be playing to half-empty houses. Robinson's aura was such he could always put bums on seats. But Buckley was adamant in his hatred.

'The guy's greedy. He squeezes you 'til the pips squeak.'

Well, that was one point of view. I liked Sugar Ray: not only was he the master craftsman of the sport, but he was also an affable companion. Only a couple of hours after he literally had been dragged out of Chicago Stadium having beaten Carmer Basilio in one of those fights you wish had been easier, we (the British Press) were invited at one o'clock in the morning to the Drake Hotel on Lakeshore Drive and ushered up to his suite.

Sugar Ray was propped up in bed, in blue-and-white striped pyjamas, his sleek hair immaculately brushed. He was so exhausted from the fight (which he won) that he could scarcely raise his voice above a whisper, but for thirty minutes, he talked. You don't forget things like that.

In the early 1970s, he was on hard times, scraping a few bucks from New York City as a Harlem youth counsellor. I asked him to come to the BBC offices on Fifth Avenue to record a TV interview. At the appointed time, the commissionaire in the lobby of the

Pioneering days of television, some time in the 1950s: W. Barrington Dalby is doing the inter-rounds. Squatting alongside is producer Humphrey Fisher, whose dad just happened to be the Archbishop of Canterbury.

Rockefeller Building phoned to say Mr Robinson had arrived and was on his way up.

The BBC offices are on the twenty-first floor. I walked out to the elevator to greet him. No elevator came. I waited on. From around the corner, where the stairwell was, I heard rapid steps. I opened the stairway door and peered down. Sugar Ray was running up the stairs. He arrived at the twenty-first floor not even out of breath. He was well into his fifties at the time. I asked what was wrong with the elevator.

'Nothing,' he said. 'When I was a kid I got trapped in one of those things. Scared the hell out of me. Never used one since.'

How do you live all your life in New York and never use a lift? Maybe that explains a lot about the character of Sugar Ray Robinson. He died all too early, in 1989, at the age of sixty-seven.

In the summer months of these salad days I made a weekly trip down to the East End of London to watch boxing on a bomb site round the corner from Mile End tube station. The matchmaker was a brash boy called Mickey Duff, in his early twenties. His real name was Morris Prager. He and his parents had fled from Poland in the 1930s when Hitler was on the rampage. He took the name Mickey Duff from a James Cagney film. When I first met him he had only recently retired as a professional boxer.

At the time, I was reading *What Makes Sammy Run?* by Budd Schulberg. Sammy Glick was a ruthless Hollywood hustler. Mickey had the same hell-bent determination to succeed. He was a regular at Solomons' gym. I listened to the way he argued with, swore at, and browbeat fight managers at least twice his age, and marked him down as a young hustler who might make his mark. I didn't know the half of it.

Jack Solomons could hear Mickey shouting his head off through the walls of his office. Jack would cock an ear, smile and say: 'That Mickey Duff . . . when will he learn to keep his voice down?' A few years later Duff was threatening Jack's supremacy as the country's number one promoter. A few years after that, Mickey *was* number one. Jack was out of business. The boy from the bomb site grew into the world's shrewdest promoter and manager. He never did learn to lower his voice.

The Queen's Coronation in 1953 lit the fuse to television's take-off in Britain. From being radio's little brother, it boomed into big business. Eamonn Andrews was no longer with me at ringside. He now fronted *What's My Line?*. He and the panel of Barbara Kelly, Lady Barnett, David Nixon and Gilbert Harding were catapulted into

I spent a lot of my professional life in the company of Eamonn Andrews, at the ringside and in the studio. Week after week we were together on Saturday's famous radio show Sports Report *and invariably wound up in the BBC Club with a glass in our hands.*

stardom. Eamonn also had a firm footing in radio, having taken over the presentation of *Sports Report* at five o'clock every Saturday evening.

His rapport with the show's hard-to-please producer, Angus Mackay, was the basis of the most successful partnership in the history of radio sport. With headphones jammed over his ears and Angus's brisk Scots voice booming through them, Eamonn virtually ran the show off the cuff. In one hour they grabbed every story of the day and frequently called in items from around the world. It was a *tour de force*, previously unmatched.

When, eventually, I took part in the same show, Eamonn and I resumed a friendship that lasted until the day he died. I worked long enough beside him to appreciate his ability. He was TV's first major star in this country and brought a special professionalism to all his work that can be sensed even today in the inherited output of the BBC and ITV.

I now did TV boxing, for the most part, alone, and in the winter we were on the air live almost every Thursday night for fifty minutes with top-class amateur internationals. We began to make our own stars. One of the first was a South London boy, Roy Francis, who skinned eels for a living in Brixton.

On an October night in 1955 he turned out at light-middleweight

for Britain against the USA at Wembley. His opponent, Frankie Davis, serving in the US Air Force, had won all his sixty-five contests, many of them in the opening round. He was the star performer in the American team. Almost at once, Davis cracked Francis with a left hook that hurled the English boy into the ropes. Davis moved in for another one-round win, at which point Francis slipped Davis's right-hand lead and let go his own right. It smacked Davis flush on the jaw. The American hit the floor with a crash and was counted out. It was all over in fifty-six seconds and Roy was a national hero. You have to remember that in those days we didn't do too well against the Americans and to see one of theirs flat on his back in this dramatic way captured the public imagination to such a degree I still get letters about it, nearly forty years on.

And then, of course, there was Dick McTaggart . . . but I'm jumping ahead. The year 1954 was another watershed for me. In

Sammy McCarthy on the way to beating Roy Ankrah, the 'Black Flash' from Ghana, at Harringay in 1954, the first fight I reported for the Daily Mail.

September, our son Clive was born and three months later I relinquished my cushy number with *Sporting Record*. The weekly column and the education in Solomons' gym were over. I joined the *Daily Mail* as their boxing writer in succession to the distinguished Geoffrey Simpson, who had died all too early some weeks previously. I just hoped I could handle it.

I had no background in daily paper journalism, no experience at all in the frantic business of getting a round-by-round report of a big fight down the phone and on to the Sports Desk literally as it happened, then coming up with the polished, rewritten effort. It amuses me now, but terrified me then that having just finished my round-by-round report, George Metcalfe, the Sports Editor, would invariably say, 'Thanks, Harry, now let's have your *considered* piece.'

My first assignment for the *Mail* at Harringay, on 7 December 1954, was a fight between Sammy McCarthy, British featherweight champion, and Roy Ankrah, the former Empire champion from Ghana whose whirlwind style resembled the antics of an exploding octopus. Sammy, only twenty-three, yet already showing signs of becoming a master craftsman, totally outboxed him over ten rounds.

For all his skill, Sammy could never reliably subdue opponents. He lacked a punch and held his British title for only a few months. Six weeks after the Ankrah win, Billy 'Spider' Kelly of Belfast took the championship from him. Sammy, a shy, smiling boy who fell into bad company, never was a major force in boxing after that, but he made his exit like a showman. He announced his retirement to Eamonn Andrews on *This Is Your Life* in 1957. I can never forget Sammy McCarthy, the first winner I ever reported for the *Daily Mail*.

3

'Feeding a Bowl of Blood to a Tiger'

Work came thick and fast after that. I covered both amateur and professional boxing for the *Mail* and very soon they had me reporting soccer, athletics and the Boat Race. There was also more television. Just before my move into Fleet Street proper, the BBC asked if I fancied doing some greyhound racing commentaries, knowing that my first job after leaving school was on a dog-racing paper.

That is how I came to be commentating on the Greyhound St Leger at Wembley in September 1954. Before the race we showed the previous week's semi-finals on film. Minutes before the off, bookmakers in London and Birmingham were besieged with phone calls from viewers who, having seen the form in the heats, now wanted to place bets on the final.

Most of them backed Pancho Villa, who had run well in the rain in his semi-final. Now it was raining again. Pancho Villa won. It was the first time bookies had been rung up on the strength of TV coverage. It made front page news in the *Daily Express* the following morning. One of Britain's biggest bookmakers, Duggie Stuart, mentioned 'at least treble our usual amount of greyhound betting, and a lot of it from people who don't usually play the dogs.' It was a clear sign. TV already had a big hold on the viewing public.

Within six months of joining the *Mail* I flew the Atlantic for the first time to report on Don Cockell's bid for the world heavyweight title held by Rocky Marciano. It was May 1955. World travel is now commonplace. No one today blinks an eyelid at the thought of a holiday in Florida, but in 1955 there were no jet flights across the Atlantic. You flew in piston-engined planes.

It took about fifteen hours from London to New York, with a stopover in Iceland or Greenland for refuelling. I was lucky. The *Mail* sent me first class, with a sleeping-berth. When bedtime came, the stewardess propped a small ladder against the berth in the rack above your seat and you climbed up to bed. A tiny pair of curtains were pulled for privacy and you curled up on the bunk. The drawback was that the moment you laid your head on the pillow the endless thrumming of the engines hit you in the ears. On the BOAC stratocruiser, the last word in aviation luxury, you not only had a bed, but also a spiral staircase that led down to a cocktail bar in the underbelly of the plane.

The Marciano-Cockell fight was in San Francisco, which meant changing planes in New York and another eight hours in the air crossing the USA from east to west. I didn't mind. You can hardly complain at seeing the Grand Canyon with a gin-and-tonic in your hand and somebody else footing the bill.

I paid in other ways. If anyone imagines covering a world heavyweight championship for a British national newspaper for the first time in your life is simple, let him try it. I was up against Peter Wilson of the *Mirror*, Desmond Hackett of the *Express*, Gerald Walter of the *News Chronicle* and George Whiting of the *Evening Standard*, all of them Fleet Street stars of the sports pages. I was being judged against them.

Whiting did me up in style. George was a cunning old pro who spoke gor-blimey English and wrote like an angel. He and I went out to Marciano's camp one day. When we got back to the St Francis Hotel, George said, 'Let's have a look at the evening papers, in case we've missed something.'

The only item relating to the fight was a tiny paragraph saying that the doctor who mended Marciano's nose after his fight with Ezzard Charles had been invited to come and watch the fight. George and I agreed there was nothing in that to get excited about. We parted company. At three o'clock in the morning I was woken by a hammering on the bedroom door. The night-porter handed me a cable from Pat Reekie, my Sports Editor in London. It read: WHITING FRONT PAGE STORY SAYS MARCIANO DOCTOR TOLD DROP EVERYTHING FLY AT ONCE STOP CHECK AND FILE STORY. I could have killed George.

I got my own back later with an exclusive about the small ring

May 1955, San Francisco, outside Don Cockell's training HQ. Left to right: *Desmond Hackett* (Daily Express), *Jack Solomons, Frank Butler* (News of the World), *Tom Phillips* (Daily Herald), *Gerald Walter* (News Chronicle), *Peter Wilson* (Daily Mirror) *and yours truly. The sign over the door was a shade optimistic. Rocky Marciano obviously hadn't read it.*

Cockell would be forced to use. It was sixteen feet square, instead of the twenty-foot ring Cockell had been promised. You needed all the space you could get when Marciano was chasing. Reekie was pleased. He cabled: CONGRATULATIONS STOP FROM NOW ON FILE FRONT PAGE STORY EVERY DAY. The terrible thing was that he meant it.

Don Cockell, a blacksmith from Battersea, had been an outstanding light-heavyweight until metabolism problems brought on excessive weight, forcing him into the heavyweight division. I knew him well. At one time he bred poodles and I bought a pup from him. We called it Champ.

Don was a skilful boxer with plenty of courage. Before the fight with Marciano, he told his manager, John Simpson: 'On no account do you throw in the towel. I'll take my chance.'

His chance with Rocky Marciano was minimal. I had never seen Marciano fight, but I knew he had come through forty-seven fights without being beaten and had won the title from Jersey Joe Walcott with one thundering blow in the thirteenth round when all had seemed lost. Everyone understood the paradox of this man. Rocky was soft-spoken and polite outside the ring. Inside it, he was merciless, unscrupulous even. Rocky would butt, thumb and elbow you without compunction. Al Weill, his manager, once said that offering Marciano money to fight was like 'feeding a bowl of blood to a tiger'.

The moment the bell rang he charged forward, throwing punches non-stop. His only concession to defence was a rudimentary crossing of the arms in front of his face, a tactic taught him by little Charley Goldman, who had been responsible for sculpting a world champion out of a slab of human granite.

Cockell lasted into the ninth round, which, by any standards, was a remarkable tribute to him. Rocky, of course, butted him, and Don butted back. But the insuperable strength and will of Marciano overcame him and the last two or three rounds were frightening as Cockell was hammered down and out of the fight.

Don was the first Briton to challenge for the title since Tommy Farr's fight with Joe Louis in 1937. Sadly, the fight in San Francisco's Kezar football stadium did not attract a big crowd and Don made no fortune from it. His career was all but over.

And so was Rocky's . . . but I didn't realise that when I made my second trip to the States four months later in September 1955. Never was there a more astonishing character in the gaudy world of boxing than Archie Moore. He had his first professional fight in 1935.

Two of the greatest fighters who ever lived: Archie Moore (left) and Rocky Marciano. In New York, 1955, Moore, forty-one, slammed Marciano to the floor in the second round and lived to regret it. It was Rocky's last fight. Ancient Archie kept going for another eight years.

Left In the Kezar football stadium, Marciano took Cockell apart in nine rounds. But he couldn't knock him out. Cockell's bravery saw to that. This happened at the end of the eighth. Don went down twice more in the ninth, but was still on his feet when the referee stopped it.

In the ensuing years he showed such prodigious talent no manager of a world champion would place his man in the same ring as Archie. Moore was forced to roam the world in search of fights. In 1940, for example, he toured Australia. He was still fighting twelve years later and still had not been given a shot at the world light-heavyweight title, although by now he had racked up almost 200 fights and lost very few of them.

In 1952 Jack 'Doc' Kearns, who had managed Jack Dempsey back in the 1920s, 'allowed' Moore to challenge Joey Maxim, his world light-heavyweight champion. Archie won, of course. We then discovered Kearns had acquired a 'piece' of Moore. Such is the way boxing deals are made.

Having won the 12st 7lb championship, Moore reckoned he now deserved a crack at the big one. He wanted Marciano. Archie told everyone who would listen that his twin assets of 'relaxism and escapology' – he talked like this – would be more than sufficient to put Rocky in his rightful place, which was on the floor.

Furthermore, by fighting at heavyweight, Archibald Lee Moore would be spared the hideous indignity of getting down to 12st 7lb. For years, Moore had put on large lumps of weight between fights. He was expert at getting it off without impairing his efficiency.

I had close evidence of this in 1956 when he came to London to fight Yolande Pompey. I sat at his table at dinner. Moore chewed every piece of meat the requisite thirty-two times and then retrieved it from his mouth, carefully depositing it on the plate. He excused himself thus: 'I know it ain't etiquette, but it's sure effective.'

Marciano's manager, Al Weill, turned the usual deaf ear to Archie's pleadings. So Moore went on a nationwide campaign to shame Rocky into fighting him. He moved into towns on fight night, dressed in Western gear, proclaimed himself 'Sheriff' and stuck up 'Wanted' posters with Marciano's photograph on them.

On 21 September 1955, Moore got his wish in New York's Yankee Stadium in front of nearly 60,000 people. 'I may sound like a braggart when I say the title is mine. I know I can beat Marciano, not because he's a bad fighter, but because I'm a better one,' said Archie. On this fateful night, Moore claimed to be thirty-eight years old, but his mother – and you felt she ought to know – said he was forty-one.

In the second round Moore let go a right half-uppercut which caught Marciano flush on the jaw. I still count it as one of the hardest punches I have seen one man land on another. Even The Rock crumbled and fell. But at two – or maybe it was three – he got up and Moore knew he couldn't win. When you've hit a man with the best punch of a long fighting life and he shakes it off, you're done for. Moore survived, courageously, into the ninth, like Cockell.

And that, we said, was that. The time had come for Archie Moore to call it a day. Instead, a few months later, Marciano announced he would never fight again, while Moore kept on fighting – and for the most part winning – until 1963. His mum said he was fifty.

Just before I headed for New York for Marciano *v* Moore I opened my *Daily Mail* (penny-ha'penny, old money) to find a virulent anti-boxing diatribe penned by Paul Gallico, the American novelist. Just to give you the flavour, this was the opening: 'I should scrap all rings, burn all boxing-gloves, and never let a youth be taught to strike another with his fist. For prize-fighting and boxing are stupid, senseless, unappetising, inefficient, and 100 per cent useless.'

From someone who had been glad to make his journalistic name in the 1920s by going into the ring with Dempsey and reporting the experience, I thought this was blatant hypocrisy. It was daunting, nonetheless, to be confronted by Arthur Wareham, the *Mail* Editor, and requested (i.e. ordered) to write a reply.

Borrowing Gallico's armoury of adjectives, I went into battle decrying his outburst as 'cruel, vicious, irresponsible, unreliable, untruthful, merciless and cynical'. Over the top? Probably, but then so was Gallico. I had another go: 'If he honestly labours under the

Daily Mail *cartoonist Illingworth pictured me thus when I came out fighting against US novelist Paul Gallico* (right)*, who wrote a vitriolic attack on boxing.*

delusion that amateur boxing doesn't do something to keep young boys off the streets and out of mischief and is not in any way a character-forming activity, he should be led once a year, forcibly if necessary, to any of the youth tournaments held in this country.'

Gallico's sweeping derogation included the statement that 'by and large boxing . . . has never added an iota to the stature of anyone as a human being worth his salt.' I could only retort that 'I should like to be around when Mr Gallico decides to air his views face to face, say, with Gene Tunney, Don Cockell, Freddie Mills, Bombardier Billy Wells, Rocky Marciano or Len Harvey.'

The Golden Gloves tournament is America's most respected amateur boxing championship. Gallico helped found it in the 1930s. Now, he said, he regretted it. I found his onslaught cheap, distorted and offensive. Yet he undoubtedly helped further my career. The anti-Gallico article impressed somebody. A few weeks later I was handed the job of *Daily Mail* sports columnist and my money was practically doubled overnight. I had just celebrated my thirtieth birthday, our son was a year old and life was looking up. I was to get £50 a week. £50! For little more than that you could buy a black-and-white fourteen-inch TV set. Colour television was still more than ten years away.

Britain's boxing writers traditionally present a Club tie to visiting world champions. We enjoyed handing one to Jack Dempsey, the old Manassa Mauler. I can always say Dempsey laid his right hand on me and I didn't feel a thing. That's Gilbert Odd, our senior boxing scribe, on the right.

Dick McTaggart, Britain's best amateur boxer of the last sixty years. He's holding his Sportsman of the Year trophy, presented to him by his own city of Dundee after winning the 1956 Olympic lightweight gold medal. He won another medal in the 1960 Olympics and was still around in the 1964 Games in Tokyo.

Dick McTaggart, amateur boxer supreme, was never seen in colour. He was one of our early TV stars, in the days when the BBC covered eight or more shows a season from Scotland and I worked for Glasgow producer Bill Stevenson. I still have – and I'm sure his family has – the miniature ring in silver and ebony the Scottish ABA handed us after we had completed fifty shows together.

McTaggart, who came from a Dundee family of boxers, had uncanny judgment on how much work was needed to win a bout. He always seemed to do just enough. He was a southpaw with no real sting behind his punches, but an awesome ability to stay out of trouble and steadily collect points. He is almost the only boxer I have seen who kept his eyes on the other man's gloves. Most boxers look each other in the eyes.

McTaggart's skills enabled him to win every major competition he entered: ABA, European, Commonwealth and Olympic Games. In 1956 the Olympics went to Melbourne, the first time they had been celebrated in the southern hemisphere. McTaggart was triumphant. He outpointed four men, including Laguetko, the Russian, and collected not only the lightweight gold, but also the Val Barker Trophy as the best stylist.

Sam Docherty, a Scottish fight manager, later called on him at his Dundee flat, dumped a stack of banknotes on the table and tried to tempt him to turn pro. Dick turned him down. He had the good sense to understand that his style was not suited to the pro game. Now he passes on his deep knowledge of the sport to young Scots amateurs.

Those Melbourne Olympics were my first. I was part of the Associated Newspapers pool headed by J.L. Manning of the *Sunday Dispatch*. Laurie Pignon of the *Sketch*, Bill McGowran and Terry O'Connor of the *London Evening News* completed the team. We all turned our hand to everything and our reports appeared in one another's papers.

Considering the money and effort spent, it was a pity not one of us knew that Gillian Sheen had won a gold medal for Britain in the fencing, but the simple – and shameful – truth was that we ignored the event because it was well known the British didn't win fencing golds.

Just as well I made a better stab at the boxing, where Britain, amazingly, won five medals. Terry Spinks, the Cockney flyweight, won our second gold. Tommy Nicholls, the Shropshire lad at featherweight, won silver. Nicky Gargano, superb stylist at welter, and John McCormack, forthright Scottish light-middle, picked up bronzes. We have never done remotely as well since.

The journey from London to Melbourne, by Qantas's piston-engined Constellation, took three and a half days with an overnight rest in Singapore. Laurie Pignon handed out sleeping pills on the first night and we stayed awake all night arguing politics and religion. He had confused the knockout drops with energy pills.

These early days on the *Mail*, overwhelming with new experiences, also took me into the High Court on a libel suit. Nothing to do with me. I didn't write the offending piece. Unhappily, the litigant was Don Cockell, whom I admired for his stand against Marciano and with whom I had struck up a friendship.

In April 1956, Cockell and his stablemate, Jack Gardner, had been drastically beaten on the same night at Earl's Court, London. Cockell was down six times and knocked out in two rounds by Kitione Lave of Tonga, while Gardner was badly cut and hammered before being stopped in two rounds by Joe Bygraves of Jamaica.

To understand the impact of this debacle, you have to realise that Cockell and Gardner had been Britain's leading heavyweights for many years. Gardner had put Bruce Woodcock into retirement back in 1950, while Cockell was still British and Empire champion. Their crushing defeats prompted a Boxing Board inquiry. Gardner's licence was taken away and Cockell had his Empire title stripped. Neither man ever fought again.

I let rip at both fighters in the *Mail*. Reading it now I am not proud of the piece, but I suppose it reflects how all of us in boxing felt at the time. The article was headlined 'Go! Go! The pair of you were a disgrace' and the text contained lines like 'You have overstayed your welcome . . . you were disgustingly fat, flabby, slow . . . overweight and undertrained.'

At the time, Britain's car workers were on strike. The *Mail*'s chief leader writer somehow equated the boxing fiasco with the strike as a sign of Britain's malaise. In a powerful (anonymous) piece on the front page he described Cockell and Gardner as 'a pair of prize layabouts who had not taken the trouble to train'.

Cockell slapped in a writ for libel. His objection was not to being called 'a prize layabout' but to the accusation that he had not bothered to train. I felt the article was indefensible. After all, I had watched him train. Whether he had trained sufficiently was another matter. But how could you say he had *not taken the trouble* to train?

However, the *Mail* decided to defend the action and retained the services of Gilbert Beyfus, QC. The solicitors told me I was their 'sheet-anchor', placing surprising faith in me as a witness as I was bound to say that I had actually seen Cockell train for the fight.

Right *Baby-faced Terry Spinks* (left), *Britain's other gold medal winner in the Melbourne Games. We've never done as well since.*

When the case came to the High Court in the Strand, Don Cockell's silk turned out to be Gerald Gardiner, later Lord Gardiner and Lord Chancellor. The presiding judge was Lord Chief Justice Goddard, well-known for his scathing dislike of the Press. The solicitors may have felt confident, but I didn't.

Under Gilbert Beyfus's examination, I explained that Cockell had been a light-heavyweight of considerable repute, but that a metabolism problem had forced him into the heavyweight division, where I regarded him as less effective.

Then came the cross-examination by Gerald Gardiner, QC: 'Mr Carpenter, do I understand you to say that my client is not as good a heavyweight as he was a light-heavyweight?'

'Yes, sir.'

'Mr Carpenter, am I correct in believing that my client won the heavyweight championship of Great Britain?'

'Yes, sir.'

'Am I also correct in thinking that my client won the heavyweight championship of the British Empire?'

'Yes, sir.'

'And of Europe?'

'Yes, sir.'

'Am I also correct in believing that my client fought for the world heavyweight championship against Mr Rocky Marciano and was generally thought to have displayed remarkable courage in lasting nine rounds with him?'

'Yes, sir.'

At this point, Lord Chief Justice Goddard, sitting immediately to my left, coughed once, turned to me, peered over his pince-nez and said softly: 'Well, Mr Carpenter, all I can say is that perhaps you're not a very good judge of these matters.'

Cockell won his case and the jury awarded him £7,500, massive damages in those days. Why Jack Gardner did not follow up and sue, I shall never know, but he didn't. In the years to come, Cockell and I remained on good terms, but he always believed I was the instigator of the libel. The man who did write it won an award in the next Honours List.

4

'Get Out There and Fight'

There were Wednesday afternoons at this time that I thought were taking years off my life. Peter Dimmock (here he comes again) was fronting a Wednesday night BBC-TV programme called *Sportsview*, the forerunner of *Sportsnight*. The editor was Paul Fox, the same chap I had worked alongside during those Saturday afternoons and evenings on the *People*.

At this time – the late 1950s – the Boxing Board still had a resolute ban on showing professional boxing live. The big London fights took place on Tuesday nights. *Sportsview* put film cameras in and then edited the material for showing on Wednesday evening. Because I was preoccupied reporting the fights for the *Daily Mail* I could not put commentary on them as they took place. So on Wednesday afternoons I hurried from Fleet Street to Lime Grove and reported to the dubbing theatre where Paul Fox and his assistants were waiting with the edited film. It was flashed up on the screen and I put an ad-libbed commentary on it.

If that sounds straightforward, I assure you it was not. In those days any mistake or hesitation in the commentary meant you had to go back to the start and begin again. You could not just pick up where you had left off. Some of these edited fights ran to forty minutes. A fluff in the final minutes meant doing the whole thing again.

What with Paul Fox yelling down the headphones, 'Come on, Harry, make it live!', and my own fear of tripping over my tongue, it

is no wonder those old commentaries sound a touch hysterical when they're revived today. I hated those Wednesday afternoons. They did no harm to Paul Fox. He became Managing Director of BBC Television.

That huge Earl's Court arena where Turpin beat Robinson and where Cockell and Gardner came to grief figured in my life again in January 1959. Henry Cooper beat Brian London there and became British heavyweight champion. I had been watching Henry box since 1952 when he won his first ABA Championship. It had taken him seven years to reach this professional pinnacle. As it happened, he was only just starting out.

In 1957 I had seen Henry knocked out in Stockholm by the Swedish heavyweight Ingemar Johansson. In 1958 Johansson sorted out Joe Erskine of Wales in thirteen rounds in Gothenburg. I saw

Hands up those who remember Sportsview. *It's 1956. On the right is the programme's editor, a young (now Sir) Paul Fox and next to him the late Geoff Dyson, straight-talking athletics coach.*

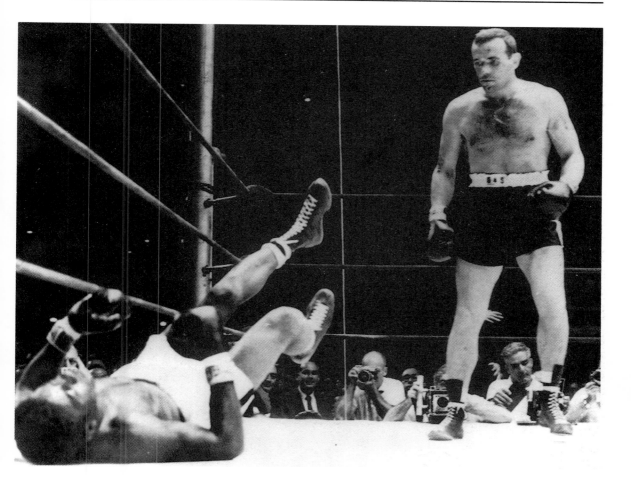

Ingemar Johansson's big right hand – 'Ingo's Bingo' – lifts the world heavyweight crown from the stricken Floyd Patterson in New York, 1959. Patterson went down seven times. Afterthought: if Ingo's Bingo was all that good, how come Patterson kept getting up?

that, too. In 1959 I flew to New York. Floyd Patterson was putting up his world title against this same Johansson in Yankee Stadium, where Moore had almost obliterated Marciano.

Just off Broadway was a ticket agency, with a loop of film on display showing Johansson's big right hand demolishing the useful American Eddie Machen in 2min 16sec the previous year. I watched that.

Then I went to Ingemar's training camp at the Jewish resort called Grossinger's in the Catskill Mountains, 100 miles north of New York City. This was where Marciano had sweated for nine months in every year. Johansson seemed to spend most of his time either playing golf or lounging by the pool. He did no real training in the six days immediately before the fight. When he did train, there was no sign of the big right hand. If you asked Ingo why he didn't throw it, he merely said: 'I don't waste it in practice. I save it for the real thing.'

Eddie Ahlquist, his manager, bought us a drink in the bar and earnestly explained to Don Saunders, of the *Telegraph*, and me how Ingo's 'toonder' (thunder) punch would destroy Patterson, the way it had destroyed Machen, Erskine and Cooper. The punch was known to the Press as 'the Hammer of Thor'.

Don and I listened politely, then went away to write our pieces, not forgetting to mention that Ingemar was sharing his Grossinger's apartment with his stunning blonde girlfriend, Birgit Lundgren. This, we explained gravely, was no way to train for a big fight. In common with the other 'experts', we tipped Patterson to win.

In the third round Johansson planted the 'toonder' punch, the Hammer of Thor, the one I'd seen embarrass Cooper, Erskine and Machen, smack on Patterson's chin. He sprawled on his back. In retrospect, it is astonishing that Patterson went down seven times in this round. If the big right was so formidable, how come Patterson got off the floor six times? After the seventh tumble, referee Ruby Goldstein called it off and we had a new champion.

Ingemar Johansson, twenty-six, in his twenty-second pro fight, was the first European to win the heavyweight championship of the world since Primo Carnera a quarter of a century earlier, and he came from a country that at that time had only six professional boxers. I knew Patterson had a weak chin. I knew Ingo had a big right. Why didn't I tip him? Don't ask. If I knew who was going to win, I wouldn't be commentating for a living.

Then came 1960: another Olympic Games – Rome this time. There Nat Fleischer, editor of America's *Ring* magazine, told me to keep an eye on a new fellow, a young light-heavyweight. 'Flashy,' says Nat, 'but with potential.'

The new chap was Cassius Clay.

Fleischer was right. Clay was *very* flashy. Extremely fast and skilful, he danced in the ring like no other big man I had seen. He was a light-heavyweight (12st 10lb) at this time. In the Olympic semi-final he faced Tony Madigan, a hard, competent Australian whose career had been pursued in London. Madigan had lost the 1953 ABA final to Henry Cooper, but won it the following year, and in Cardiff in 1958, he won the Empire Games gold medal. He was good, but Clay outpointed him. Tony always claimed it was a bad decision. It was certainly close.

In the final Clay met Zbigniew Pietrzykowski, a phlegmatic Pole, unquestionably the best amateur light-heavy in Europe. No British

Olympic Games, Rome, 1960. Cassius Clay wins the light-heavyweight gold by outsmarting brilliant Polish southpaw, Zbigniew Pietrzykowski, champion of Europe. No one imagined Clay, who changed his name to the Islamic Muhammad Ali, would one day be heavyweight champion of the world. But here was Clay ready to be moulded into greatness.

boxer had ever beaten him. Cassius toyed with him, opened up cuts all over his face and swept to victory without being troubled. That was impressive.

Smartly stylish though his performance was, Clay did not win the coveted Val Barker award Dick McTaggart had collected four years earlier in Melbourne as the outstanding technical boxer. It went to Nino Benvenuti, the Italian welterweight. As Nino later won world professional titles at two weights, I suppose it doesn't do to complain. As for McTaggart, he collected a bronze at lightweight in these Rome Olympics, which underlines how brilliant he was over a long period. Cassius Clay went home to the States and I thought no more of him . . . for a while.

As the 1960s opened, British professional boxing was enjoying the exploits of Dave Charnley and Terry Downes. Charnley, from Dartford in Kent, with Scottish ancestry, was a chunky lightweight who, in a 1954 ABA final, had stopped Dick McTaggart inside a round, which tells you something.

Chat with Charnley at Belle Vue, Manchester. Lightweight Dave from Dartford, Kent, was one of the best British fighters never to win the world title. An old Brown man got in his way: Joe Brown of the USA. Dave lost to him twice. When he did beat him, Joe no longer held the title.

Left Clay, Olympic champion, with the gold medal he later threw into a river in protest against white racism. Pietrzykowski the Pole occupies the number two position. The bronze medallists are Giulio Saraudi of Italy and Tony Madigan of Australia, who boxed with success in Britain.

Dave would certainly have won the world lightweight title but for an ageing American negro called Joe 'Old Bones' Brown. Charnley had two goes at him: in Houston, Texas, where an eye injury ruled him out in the fifth round, and later in London, where the referee, Tommy Little, came up with a decision for Brown after fifteen rounds. I thought Charnley had won.

Ironically, when Brown was no longer champion, they met for a third time in Manchester and Dave knocked him out. Brown was part of that superb triumvirate of negro fighters, all in action at this time: Robinson, Moore and Brown. Charnley should have arranged to be born later.

Some current British boxers with nothing like Charnley's talents win mocked-up 'world' titles. Professional boxing today is debased: too many weights, too many titles. Television, mainly in the USA, is to blame with its insatiable demand for 'meaningful' fights, together with the mushrooming of so-called 'world-governing' bodies, none prepared to give way to the others. As I write there are no fewer than sixty-four alleged world champions spread over seventeen weights. Fifty years ago there were eight champions at eight weights and we knew and respected them.

I first came across Terry Downes in the late 1950s after reading of his amateur boxing triumphs with the US Marine Corps. He had emigrated to the States with his sister, a circus trapeze artist. He returned to Britain when she lost an arm in a horrifying accident. I found him in his grandmother's basement flat in Paddington. He was barely twenty years old, but spoke in an outlandish mixture of Cockney-American with an assurance that spilt over into arrogance.

He told me US fight gyms were packed with unknown, struggling boxers who would wipe the floor with British champions. Hoarse with scorn, he insisted that once he turned pro he would be British middleweight champion within twenty fights. I went back to the *Mail* office and wrote a piece about this brash and boastful upstart who had better justify his words . . . or else. He had his first pro fight in April 1957, and in number twenty, eighteen months later, duly became British middleweight champion. I never doubted anything he said again.

On his way to becoming champion of the world Downes suffered two significant defeats. In his third pro fight he was matched by Mickey Duff with a raw Nigerian fighter, Dick Tiger, based in Liverpool. They met in that cockpit of East End boxing, Shoreditch Town Hall.

The fight was derided as a 'pushover' for Downes. Tiger was 4–1 against, but in six rounds he closed Terry's right eye, slashed a cut across the bridge of his nose and stuck him on the floor three times, at which point Downes's handlers yanked him out.

The story of Dick Tiger was a painful lesson for British boxing and bore out everything Downes had said. Strong and durable, he languished for years in Liverpool as just another fighter earning meagre rewards. It wasn't until he was taken to the States by Jersey Jones, a shrewd American manager, that his potential was realised and he rose to become middle and light-heavyweight champion of the world. As Downes himself won the world middleweight title, the match at Shoreditch in 1957, on which scorn was poured, must now be seen as the shrewdest investment Duff ever made: 'I paid £250 for the pair of them.'

Oddly Downes was put into another fight he couldn't handle in

Terry Downes is one of the outstanding British fighters of my time. In 1962, after he'd lost the world middleweight title, he beat Sugar Ray Robinson at Wembley. Spare a thought for Robinson. This was eleven years after the Turpin defeat . . . and he was still slugging out a living in the ring.

1958, shortly after he won the British title. Jack Solomons matched him at Wembley with Ellsworth ('Spider') Webb from Chicago. As Webb had been seen in London only six months earlier outpointing Dick Tiger, he was clearly a competent fighter.

Webb's right hand dropped Downes less than a minute into the fight. Humiliating defeat stared Terry in the face. From that point, however, Downes in this one fight displayed all the qualities of courage, skill, defiance and pride which eventually won him a world crown – almost two. In blazing fashion, Downes came close to forcing Webb out of the fight, but at the end of the eighth, Eugene Henderson, the man who had declared Turpin winner over Robinson, withdrew Downes because of cuts above and below his eyes.

When I came to write Terry's life story for the *Mail* I asked him what on earth had persuaded him to accept Webb as an opponent at that stage in his career. He said: 'Solomons asked me who would I prefer: Sugar Ray Robinson or Spider Webb? It was like being asked if I wanted to be shot or hung.'

Downes became world champion in the same Wembley ring some two and a half years later when he beat the Boston fireman, Paul Pender, having lost to Pender on cuts a few months earlier.

In April 1962, he went back to Boston for a third match with the American and lost. He was twenty-six, but his career was far from over. Less than six months later he outpointed the ageing Sugar Ray Robinson, still fighting eleven years after the Turpin defeat. And Downes went on winning, at the same time gaining weight.

In November 1964, we all went to Manchester to see if Terry could wrest the world light-heavyweight title from the amiable, highly-skilled Willie Pastrano from New Orleans, who could charm women as neatly as he handled opponents. After ten rounds Downes was all but champion. Pastrano could barely summon the strength to drag himself back to his stool and was close to submission. In his corner, however, was a man accustomed to breathing new life into flagging fighters.

Angelo Dundee, ace American trainer, shouted several four-letter words into Pastrano's ear, hauled him bodily off his stool at the start of the eleventh, gave him a vicious swipe across the seat of his pants and yelled: 'Get out there and fight, you dumb . . . !'

Unhappily for Downes, it worked. Pastrano switched from compliant victim to savage avenger. He smashed into Downes, floored him twice, and the fight was stopped. Terry never fought again.

Downes was as good a British fighter as I have seen. He justified every word of that youthful tirade in the Paddington basement. Although his career was blighted by cuts, notably to his 'hooter', as he called it, he never complained. In fact, he labelled his autobiography *My Bleeding Business* with appealing black humour.

He probably never received due credit for his boxing ability. I once watched him completely outbox Joey Giardello, a tough American thought to be pretty skilful. Terry has a heart of gold and never rejects a call for help. I rate Mr Downes extremely highly.

Thursday, 2 November 1961 . . . a night I can never forget. I went on the air for BBC-TV at 9.25 with the news that a team of US amateur boxers had so far failed to record a win in their match at Wembley with Great Britain. When I came off the air an hour or so later, the nation had seen the Americans whitewashed . . . 10–0!

It was the match, of course, in which heavyweight Billy Walker slung a right and a left to the jaw of 6ft 3in Cornelius Perry, a 17st baker from Philadelphia, and left him flat on his back, badly concussed, after 1min 54sec of the opening round.

Right *Golden boy Billy Walker blasting out the huge black American, Cornelius Perry, on the night in '61 when Great Britain thumped the USA 10–0. Billy's success this night and his subsequent TV popularity enabled brother George to found the Brent Walker financial empire.*

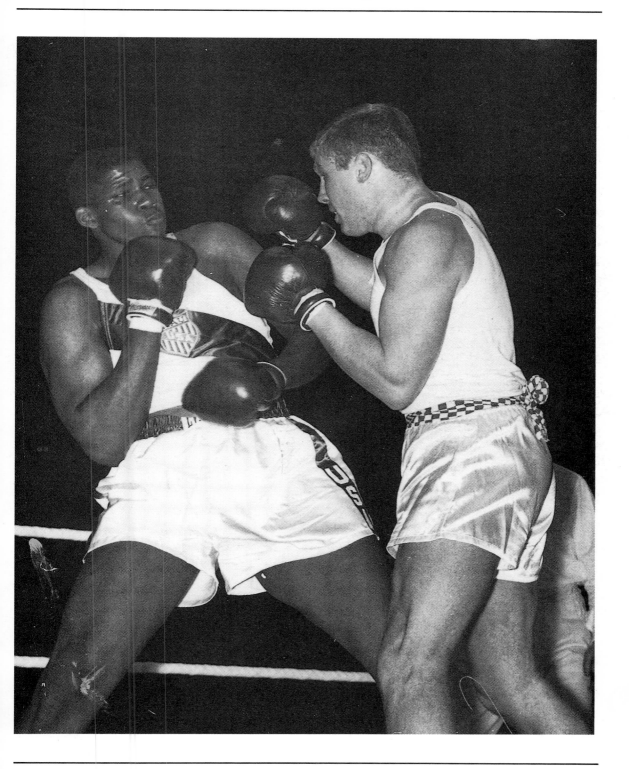

Top men from the days when I wrote about athletics: Herb Elliott, (left), the brilliant Australian who won the Olympic 1,500 metres in Rome, breaking his own world record, and Gordon Pirie, the controversial British athlete, who suffered two crushing defeats from the Russian Vladimir Kuts, in the Olympic 5,000 and 10,000 metres of 1956.

Few people in the history of boxing have thrown more golden punches than the couple Billy let fly on that famous night. From those blows sprang instant fame, a lucrative pro career, a thriving business launched on the profits by brother George Walker, which in turn grew into the Brent-Walker financial empire. Brother George became one of the country's high-flying City tycoons and Billy, the Golden Boy of British boxing, took up comfortable retirement at an early age in the Channel Islands.

Those who saw the 10–0 win on TV invariably recall that Walker's crushing victory completed the rout. In fact, Billy's contest was seventh, at the request of the BBC, and the man, an unsung hero to this day, whose responsibility it was to complete the whitewash, was Derek Richards, a Welsh light-middleweight from Coventry. His opponent, Roy McMillan, from Toledo, Ohio, was hit so hard in the body he wound up in Wembley General Hospital with suspected

Derek Ibbotson, a barrel-chested Yorkshireman, hits the tape at White City, London, in July 1957 and breaks the world mile record in 3 min 57.2 sec. Those were the days when sub-four-minute miles were still news.

broken ribs, alongside Walker's opponent and one or two other members of the American team.

There were superb performances that night from Britain's inspired team. Frankie Taylor, who later became 'Tiger' Taylor as a pro and today writes about the game, chopped Ralph Ungricht, eighteen, from Utah, nose down into the ring dust in the final round.

Dick McTaggart (yes, he was there) did his usual points job on Woodie Marcus, America's national champion. Leotis Martin, American middleweight, who later became a respected heavyweight pro (he KO'd Sonny Liston), was put out of action in the final round by one mighty southpaw left to the stomach from Scots miner John Fisher. It doubled Martin in half and left him gasping in agony.

Jim Caldwell, a Wisconsin Indian from the Menominee tribe, entered the ring wearing full Red Indian head-dress, plus purple warpaint on his shoulders. It did not overawe British soldier Brian

Brazier. Alan Rudkin, who would later fight three times for a world title, got off the floor in the opening round to stop seventeen-year-old Sherman Washington in the third.

Having completed the BBC stint and written my story for the *Mail*, I then went to Wembley General, where half the US team were taken as casualties. I could have done with a sick bed myself. I got through the evening by swallowing codeine tablets to deaden the pain of shingles, which had broken out over my head. It was the second 'stress' illness I'd had in just over a year. In 1960 I was out of action for six weeks with infective hepatitis, or jaundice.

I was over-working and the time had come to simplify matters. Peter Dimmock, the man who produced my first TV commentary in 1949, was now the BBC's Head of Outside Broadcasts and for some time had been urging me to make TV my full-time occupation. He sent me a sample contract which was not appealing.

The relationship with Eamonn Andrews again came in useful. Eamonn's business manager, Teddy Sommerfield, agreed to represent me and made a better deal with the BBC. In the summer of '62 I ended eight years with the *Mail* and bade farewell to Fleet Street.

They had been good, productive years. I had had my own daily column pompously called 'I Have My Say' in which I could lay down the law about any sport I cared to name. I had met and written about such diverse characters as Chris Brasher, Herb Elliott, Dorothy Hyman, Col Frank Weldon, the Nawab of Pataudi, Gordon Pirie, Roger Bannister, Reg Harris, Edward Hide, Stanley Matthews and Colin Cowdrey.

5

Sprinting Through Mexico City

Would I have as interesting a time with the Beeb? I needn't have worried. I'd hardly been there a day or two before Bryan Cowgill, editor of *Grandstand*, the hugely successful Saturday show, asked if I would take over as presenter while David Coleman had a break. 'Come to the studio on Saturday,' he said, 'and watch how David operates.'

I knew enough to understand that the four-hour programme was a technical marvel, moving around the country to pick up any number of sports, fast-moving, complex, and a test of the presenter's ability to ad-lib his way out of tight corners. What I didn't know was whether I could handle it. Here we were in 1962, back to 1949, diving in at the deep end again. The same rule applied: having come this far, you don't back out.

So I turned up that Saturday. Between two horse races, Coleman pulled me in front of camera and told the viewers: 'This is the fellow who's taking my place for the next couple of weeks.' Then to me: 'Take your coat off.'

Bill Adams, the floor manager, appeared with a pocket receiver, an earpiece and a pin-on mike. 'This is how you'll be wired up,' said David. Bill stuck the receiver in my back trouser pocket, fixed the mike to my tie and made me insert the earpiece.

'Can you hear the producer?' asked Coleman. I nodded apprehensively. 'Good,' said David. 'You might as well have a practice. Introduce the next race.' And he walked off and left me.

Above *His little legs never touched the floor! I'm sitting on the desk of* Grandstand, *the Saturday TV sports programme I fronted from Lime Grove in the mid-1960s. That big screen was hi-tech in those days.*

I'm not sure why I was looking so supercilious. The picture, though, gives a fair impression of the paraphernalia a TV commentator has around him, not to mention the 'deaf-aid' stuck in his ear, through which the producer can talk to him. The monitor-screen is showing what engineers call 'Chinese boxes' – a picture within a picture within a picture, etc.

In September, I flew to Chicago. Floyd Patterson, who had become the first man to regain the world heavyweight title, was defending it against the most intimidating fighter I have met: Charles 'Sonny' Liston. Liston, already into his thirties, had been beaten only once in his pro career, a points defeat in a fight where his jaw had been broken in the opening round. Liston's lurid youth was spent in St Louis, Missouri, where he amused himself beating up cops and they responded with equal pleasure. He was a brooding hulk with sullen face, menacing eyes and fists which measured 16 inches in circumference.

People tell me that deep down he had a sense of humour. I never discovered it. I was too busy being scared of him. So, presumably, was Patterson. Their . . . fight? . . . took place in Comiskey Park, the Chicago home of the White Sox baseball team, where Joe Louis had begun his long tenure of the championship in 1937. Louis had taken eight rounds to beat James J. Braddock. This one was all over in 2min 6sec, the third fastest heavyweight championship in history.

Three punches did the trick: a left hook to the side of Patterson's head, a follow-up right to the chin and, as Floyd began to fall, a left to the jaw. The man who got up seven times before losing to Johansson was now groping drunkenly on all fours as Frank Sikora counted ten. Quick as it was, I cannot say I was too surprised. Liston had merely transferred his menace to his place of work. At this moment Sonny Liston was the most destructive heavyweight I had ever set eyes upon – and that included Marciano.

This fight completed a neat professional double. In 1957, in company with the omnipresent Peter Dimmock, I had commentated on the European amateur boxing championships from Prague, the first TV sports transmission from behind the Iron Curtain. Now, in Chicago, I had done the first satellite TV sports broadcast from the USA to Britain.

For ten months, neither Liston nor Patterson fought. Then we all trooped off to Las Vegas in July 1963 for the re-match. Liston's reputation as 'the Bad Man of Boxing' was reinforced when forty minutes after the set time for the weigh-in he still hadn't turned up. A 100-dollar fine was imposed on the spot with the threat of an extra 100 dollars for every further five minutes' delay. At this point Liston appeared.

When fight-time came, celebrities like Joe Louis, Rocky Marciano and Billy Conn were introduced from the ring. Then came the announcement: 'Cassius Clay!' This sleek, handsome, impeccably-dressed young man eased through the ropes, went to Patterson's

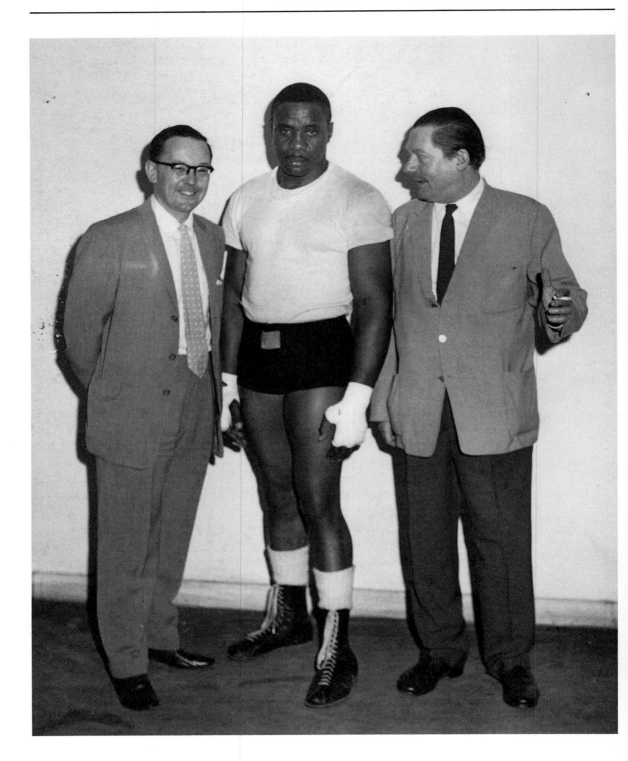

Floyd Patterson always seemed to be falling down . . . he's losing his title to Sonny Liston at Comiskey Park, Chicago, 1962. It was all over in 126 seconds. No wonder Liston was considered the number one menace of his time.

Left *My old mate from the* Mirror, *Peter Wilson ('The Man They Cannot Gag'), and I pay our respects to Sonny Liston, heavyweight champion at the time. Liston was considered unbeatable. You can tell how delighted he was to meet us.*

corner and shook hands. He turned towards Liston, took two steps, then shook his head and left the ring. Liston looked angry and had only one way to vent it, on the unfortunate Patterson. To be fair, Floyd did better this time. He lasted four seconds longer.

Since World War II many professional boxing champions have founded their success on Olympic gold. Patterson did. He was middleweight champion at the 1952 Helsinki Games, emphasising how small he was. Today's heavyweight champions come to scale at 15 stone and over. Liston was in this category and moved us into the era of mammoth champions. Patterson, Johansson, Marciano and Louis would probably fight today in the cruiserweight class (up to 13st 13lb) which did not exist twenty years ago.

The Olympic Games of Tokyo, 1964, disclosed a man who would figure in some of the most memorable nights of my life ringside. Despite a broken thumb, Joe Frazier won his final against Hans Huber of Germany. Joe didn't impress as a future heavyweight champion of the world, but then neither did Clay in 1960.

People delight in telling you how they 'spotted' so-and-so back in his amateur days. They kid themselves. About the only man I knew for sure was destined for professional stardom after Olympic gold

That label on the lapel says 'WORKING PRESS'. I'm ringside with Joe Louis, greatest heavyweight champion of them all. It's 1964 and we're trying to make sense of what we've just seen in the Miami Beach Convention Hall. Muhammad Ali, 7–1 outsider, has lifted Joe's old crown from the head of Sonny Liston. Impossible!

was Sugar Ray Leonard. The money-men could hardly wait for him to collect his medal before they began manoeuvring him to the top.

Who could honestly claim they foresaw the bizarre future of George Foreman the night he won his heavyweight gold in Mexico City, 1968? And yet George even then was adroitly working on the American psyche. He waved a miniature Stars and Stripes from the Olympic rostrum. With Muhammad Ali in disgrace at the time and America needing patriotic assurance about its Vietnam involvement, George's move was shrewd and never forgotten.

I didn't much ponder on it at the time. I had other things to think about. Less than an hour earlier Chris Finnegan of England had skilfully boxed his way to the middleweight gold, Britain's first Olympic boxing triumph since the days of Spinks and McTaggart twelve years before. BBC-TV urgently required him in their Mexico City studios for an interview. The satellite had been booked at thousands of pounds an hour and if you didn't get on it before it whistled out of range, the money was down the drain and London would hop with rage.

It was producer Bob Duncan's job to get Chris and me from the Coliseo boxing arena to the studios before the satellite disappeared. I have to say of Bob, one of my dearest friends, that few things in his professional life ever seemed to go simply and this night was no exception.

As Bob moved in to collect Chris Finnegan from the winner's rostrum, so did the doctors. Finnegan had been picked at random for a drugs test. Would he kindly accompany them to the dressing-rooms where he would be required to make water? Duncan seethed with impatience, but there wasn't a lot he could do about it.

Unfortunately Chris, dehydrated from his gold-winning efforts, was unable to summon the required sample. Taps were turned on to encourage him. We all wished him well. But nothing. Duncan was beside himself. He yelled at the men in white coats: 'I have to get Señor Finnegan to the television studios. Very important interview. To London. *Compree?*' They did not.

'Television,' screamed Bob. 'Satellite. *Mucho dinaro!*' I was afraid he might have a heart attack. Chris Finnegan still could not provide the goods. With an embarrassed, forlorn boxer on the one hand and a demented TV producer on the other, the doctors at length relented. Señor Finnegan could go to the studios, but . . . they would have to accompany him. The sample was still required.

We were now close to cut-off time for the satellite. There was no time to summon a cab. Duncan decided we would have to run the half-mile or so to the studios. We set off through the dark streets of Mexico City: Finnegan at the fore, track-suited, gold medal swinging from his neck; Duncan manfully keeping pace and apologising all the while for putting our newest Olympic champion through such indignities; two men in white coats, one clutching a specimen bottle; and me, bringing up the rear, wondering if I'd have enough breath left to conduct the interview.

We swept through the doors of Mexican TV. The studio, naturally, was upstairs. We ran up. We got on the air. The interview was done. Immediately the men in white coats grabbed Chris and led him to the men's room. Five minutes later they all reappeared. The bottle was still empty.

Finnegan now had a date with Britain's boxing officials who had planned a celebration dinner at a downtown restaurant. We were all invited, including the men in white coats. Chris was seated in the place of honour, centre of the top table. He was handed a pint of Mexican beer. Someone else gave him a big cigar. He ate, drank and puffed. At 2 am Chris pushed his chair back from the table, beamed hugely and said to the men in white coats: 'I think I'm ready to go now.'

The sample was negative, thank God.

6

'Float Like a Butterfly, Sting Like a Bee'

In March 1961, six months after the Rome Olympics, I opened a copy of the American magazine *Saturday Evening Post*, and there on page 36 Dick Schaap had written a piece headlined 'The Happiest Heavyweight'. A picture showed Cassius Clay in Rome, wearing his gold medal, being admired by a gaggle of giggling Italian girls. Another showed him at home in Louisville, Kentucky, with his parents and brother Rudy. Clay was holding up a mock newspaper he'd bought in a penny arcade in New York on his way back from the Games. The blazing headline, which he'd invented, read: CASSIUS SIGNS FOR PATTERSON FIGHT.

The Schaap article began: 'Cassius Marcellus Clay Jr, who at eighteen won the 1960 Olympic light-heavyweight boxing championship, has not the slightest doubt that he is the future heavyweight champion of the world.' Further on Clay was quoted as saying: 'I dream about what it's gonna be like. I'll have a hundred-thousand-dollar home and a beautiful wife. And I'll own two Cadillacs, and then I'll have a Ford for just getting around in. Then someday I'll own a pretty Cassius Clay hotel in Louisville and, if business is good, I'll branch out into New York and California.'

Young fighters, even Olympic champions, don't normally talk like this. Clay was clearly unusual. The article displayed a less boastful side to his nature. On his way home from Rome, he went to Sugar Ray Robinson's Harlem café for a glimpse of the great man and came

I Am The Greatest! As the years went by, the boast seemed more and more like the truth.

away delightedly clutching a signed photo. 'I'm gonna be like him,' he said. 'Sugar Ray's something. Everybody knows who he is.'

More and more people were getting to know who Clay was. He composed doggerel predicting his wins:

> *If he likes to mix, I'll let it go to six.*
> *If he wants to jive, I'll cut it to five.*
> *And if he talks some more, I'll beat him in four.*

He was right, again and again. The elegant gliding footwork and dropped hands, which Nat Fleischer and I had condemned as flashy, were, he claimed, the authentic style of the jet-age. 'All you writers are used to seeing heavyweights with slow hands and feet [he was right there] but I'm up on my toes and . . . D-A-A-A-NCING, man!' Then the clincher: 'I am The Greatest!!'

In 1963 Jack Solomons pulled off one of his last great coups: he signed Clay to come to London to fight Henry Cooper. But before that, in Madison Square Garden, Clay would meet Doug Jones, a useful fighter from New York who had recently gone the distance with Harold Johnson for the world light-heavy title. BBC-TV decided

Muhammad Ali always found time to sign autographs for fans. He had only just become champion at this time.

to buy the Clay-Jones fight and I went to New York to prepare a preview.

I had never interviewed Clay. I rang him at his hotel and put a proposition to him: 'You call yourself The Greatest. Why don't you come with me to the top of the Empire State Building. We can talk there and tell people that The Greatest has met The Highest.' The Empire State, at over 1,100 feet, was at that time the tallest building in the world. Clay loved the idea. So on that narrow windswept balcony high above New York City I did the first of I-don't-know-how-many interviews with the man who was to figure so enjoyably in my life for the best part of twenty years.

He beat Jones, of course, although it wasn't easy, and in June came to London. He was a smash hit from the moment he landed. I had seen nothing like it in the way of adulation since the days when Sugar Ray Robinson came to fight Randolph Turpin. The moment he walked on to a street, he was mobbed. And, remember, he was not champion of the world at this time. He had fought just eighteen pro fights. He was twenty-one years old. 'If he wants to jive, he'll fall in five . . .' was his prophecy for Cooper.

He didn't please everybody with his antics. *Boxing News* in its preview said: 'Henry Cooper will be doing millions of fight fans the world over a big favour if he manages to halt the upward trend of big-talking Clay . . . the Louisville Lip has, with his pathetic poetry and degrading insults to the British champ, turned everybody into a Cooper fan and will have 50,000 people roaring for his defeat.' Expert opinion at this time branded Clay a freak boxer whose come-uppance could not long be delayed. That opinion was damn near proved right at Wembley.

The weigh-in at the London Palladium provided Clay with another showman's opportunity. Backstage in a props basket he found a cardboard crown. He wore it to the scales and he wore it at Wembley, the self-proclaimed king.

Solomons and comedian Bud Flanagan come between Henry Cooper and Cassius Clay in London before their 1963 clash. Clay has one of Solomons' famed 'torpedo' cigars between his lips. It didn't stop him talking.

Left Cassius Clay – not yet world champion – proclaims himself king of the ring at Wembley. He found the crown among the props backstage at the Palladium during the weigh-in before the Cooper fight.

Oops! Henry's Hammer – the good old left hook – catches up with Clay's chin in the fourth.

It was a foul night. The infield of Wembley Stadium was a quagmire on that June evening of '63. Solomons always boasted he could control the weather at his outdoor shows. Once, in Cardiff, when Ronnie James tried to lift the world lightweight crown off Ike Williams, the rain threatened to postpone the show. Solomons summoned the Press to his hotel suite the day before the fight, stuck a bucket on the balcony and announced: 'When that pail is full, gentlemen, the rain will stop and the show will go on.' I wasn't there, but legend has it that the bucket filled, the rain stopped . . . and James lost.

There was no way Solomons could call the Wembley show off. Luckily the rain did stop. Jack hired lorryloads of duckboards and laid them on the pitch so the rich and famous could walk in comparative comfort to their six-guinea ringsides.

The *Boxing News* plea for Clay to get his come-uppance almost came off. Not, however, in front of 50,000 people. The weather kept

many at home. About 18,000 turned up and they have never forgotten what they saw. In round four, Henry's famous left hook curved out and coincided very neatly with the overworked jaw of Cassius Clay. The Greatest sprawled on his bottom in an undignified heap. Had Henry hit him with it a minute earlier, boxing history would have changed. Our 'Enry was a good finisher. But Clay was lucky. He beat the count, and before Henry could whack him again the bell ended the round.

You will now expect me to lay bare the scandalous facts: how Clay was given five minutes to recover; how Angelo Dundee magicked a razorblade from his kit and sliced one of Clay's gloves, so forcing a replacement to be sent for. You won't get that stuff from me. Yes, the interval did last more than a minute (1min 40sec, to be exact). Yes, a new glove was sent for. But, no, I don't believe Angelo slit the old one. A photograph taken during round *four* clearly shows some stuffing bursting out of Clay's glove.

Naturally, the American trainer made the most of the split. He wouldn't be worth his hire if he hadn't. Not for the last time, he helped save a fight for Clay. By the time Clay was re-gloved the eyes had stopped rolling, the brain had cleared and, in round five, just as he said he would, he forced Henry out of the fight by worsening the damage over Cooper's left eye.

That near-disaster at Wembley reinforced what most of us thought. If Clay were allowed to face Liston, the one-time convict from St Louis, Missouri would splatter him all over the ring. Hard to believe now, but Clay was still more or less a laughing-stock to the experts. They had never encountered a heavyweight who moved and talked as he did.

He used to push his nose sideways, mangle an ear with the other hand, make himself deliberately ugly, then put on a punch-drunk Brooklyn accent: 'Dis is de sort of heavyweight champ youse guys are used to seeing. Dese guys can't box like me, dey can't talk like me.' Then he'd drop the acting, dance around on his toes, shadowbox gracefully and sing out joyfully: 'Look at me. Ah'm PRETTY! Ain't nobody can box like me. Man, ah'm so PRETTY!' Ageing fight reporters, particularly Americans who had come up through the cynical Mafia days of boxing in the States, would turn away in disgust.

Clay just went on babbling merrily: 'I'm a jet-age fighter. I move, I dance, I'm light on my feet, I keep pop-popping away with my jab. Pow! Pow! Pow!' If you were close enough he'd send a left hand snaking a millimetre away from your nose. 'Man, wake up. This is the

Left *The most famous picture in modern British boxing: Cassius Clay on the seat of his pants. Our 'Enry will never be forgotten for this supreme moment in his long career. If the bell hadn't come soon after this, boxing history might have been different.*

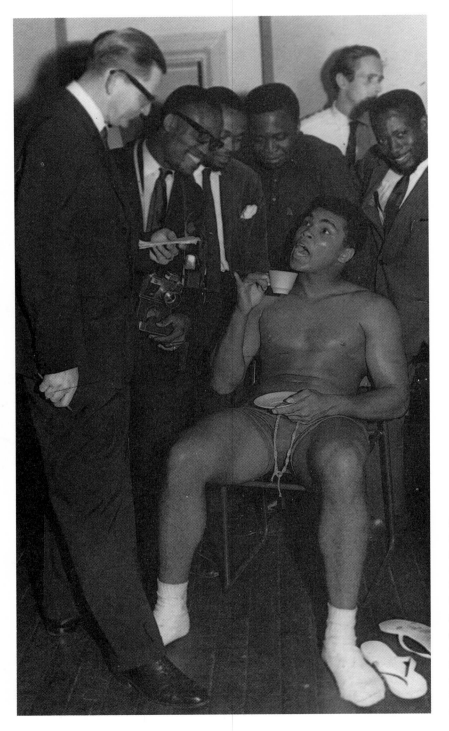

Clay won the fight with Cooper in the fifth, on a cut-eye stoppage. Now he's back in the dressing-room telling us he wasn't really worried. The big fellow with glasses, giving Clay a grilling, is Steve Fagan of the Daily Sketch. *We used to call him Inspector Fagan of the Yard, even though his work was measured in column inches.*

jet age! Them bums can't beat me. I am The Greatest!' Then he would dissolve in laughter and you'd laugh with him. I'd go off for a drink with the other writers, we'd shake our heads and deplore the terrible fate that awaited him at the hands of Sonny Liston.

Clay was the younger son of a middle-class family from Louisville, Kentucky. His father was a signwriter with a touch of artistry in him; his mother was lighter-skinned, Grady was her maiden name. Cassius Marcellus Clay took his name from a nineteenth-century US ambassador to Russia who earned a reputation for liberalism by setting free his plantation slaves. Cassius's brother had been christened Rudolph Valentino. Could you blame him for wanting to change it? It was Rudy who became a Black Muslim, changed his name to Rahman Ali, then persuaded his younger brother to join the sect. Cassius Clay became Muhammad Ali and you quickly learned never to refer to what he called his slave-name.

Charles 'Sonny' Liston seemed impregnable. His delinquent background and brooding menace, his contemptuous dismissal of Patterson in two farcically short fights, combined to make him appear as formidable a champion as there had ever been.

He had a training routine that rooted me to the spot. For a lumbering giant, he was an adept skipper. A good man with the rope can turn a training discipline into showbiz. Long before, I'd seen Eric Boon skip. He had a rhythm and agility that dazzled. But it was innocuous, almost delicate stuff. Liston's routine was pure jungle. Savage. It typified the man. He skipped to a primitive driving rock beat that speared right through you. I had never heard of James Brown and the Famous Flames. I had never heard of *Night Train*. Liston flipped the switch that triggered the tape, twirled the rope in time to the beat and then began thudding his big feet, one-two, one-two, on the dirty floorboards.

The music was straight out of the Deep South where Charles Liston had his origins. It reeked of slavery and white man's sin. I watched the sweat drip from Sonny's face and soggy singlet. It splashed in tiny drops at first, but then as he thudded, one-two, one-two, it stained the boards beneath him.

On and on he went, slapping the wet rope against the floor, lifting his thighs, pounding his feet, chest heaving, face contorted, teeth bared. It was orgasmic. The wailing music drove him on. I had my cameraman and sound engineer record every bit of it. I knew that back in London they would build the story round him. It made the point. How could a crazy, lackaday kid like Clay handle an ogre of this dimension?

I think I interviewed Liston for TV just the once. That was enough. He didn't like being quizzed. I suppose there was plenty to hide. I vividly remember the day I *did* interview him. It was before he was due to fight Patterson in Chicago. Young, innocent Cassius was mouthing off even then about what he'd do to Sonny if they ever met: 'I'll kill the big, ugly bear . . . I'll whup his ass . . .' Clay never was one for tact.

I sat down with Liston and looked into those terrible eyes. He didn't have whites of eyes. He had yellows. The eyes glared at you with sullen, shocking menace, daring you to put a question. I took my time working round to the obvious one, hoping he might soften. Some hope.

'Sonny, there's this young fighter called Cassius Clay . . .'

I paused. Maybe he'd respond. The eyes just kept mocking me.

'Do you know what Clay's saying about you?'

The eyes – that awful yellow – went on glaring.

'He's saying that if you ever meet . . . he's going to whup you.' I did not dare say 'whup your ass'. The BBC would never allow it. I also thought Liston might kill me.

The eyes didn't move off my face. He didn't speak. I thought, 'He's not even going to answer me.' Then the eyes blinked. He grunted. And from somewhere deep down in the South this rusty voice cranked out:

'You ever heard the expression whistling in the graveyard?'

The yellow eyes were challenging now. I said yes I had.

'Know what it means?'

I said I did.

'Tell me what it means.'

I was glad I hadn't tried to kid him.

'It's what somebody does when they're scared . . . they sort of whistle to keep their courage up.'

The yellow eyes ground into me.

'Yeah,' he said. 'Yeah, that's Clay. You unnerstand?'

I certainly did. I wasn't sure Clay did.

Eamonn Andrews was one of the few who tipped Clay to win. He and I were in Miami Beach for the fight. I helped him put *Sports Report* on the air from a Miami studio two days before the fight. Eamonn was convinced Clay had the ability to outbox Liston. I tried to talk him out of it. I didn't want my old friend to fall on his face in public.

Clay's poetry was getting longer. He had one for Liston:

Clay swings with a left, Clay swings with a right.
Just look at young Cassius carry the fight.
Liston keeps backing but there's not enough room.
It's a matter of time 'til Clay lowers the boom.
Then Clay lands with a right – what a beautiful swing –
The punch raises Liston clear out of the ring.
Liston's still rising – the ref wears a frown –
He can't start counting 'til Liston comes down.
Liston disappears and the crowd's getting frantic.
But our radar stations have picked him up somewhere over the
*   Atlantic.*
Who on earth thought when they came to the fight
That they'd witness the launch of a human satellite?
The crowd did not dream when they laid down their money
That they would see a total eclipse of Sonny.

Clay came to the weigh-in waving a stick, yelling, 'I'm gonna kill the big, ugly bear.' He made as if to set on Liston there and then. Handlers struggled to hold him back. He seemed to be hysterical. He was fined on the spot for misbehaviour and the doctor who examined him told us gravely: 'Clay shows all the signs of a man half-scared to death. He may not even show up for the fight.'

It was all an act. He showed up all right in the Miami Beach Convention Hall. There was nothing conventional about the fight. In round five Clay started blinking, then pawed at his eyes as if he were having trouble seeing. Back in the corner, he told Angelo: 'Get me out of here. I can't see. Something's hurting my eyes. He's got something smeared on his gloves. I don't wanna go on.'

Angelo was getting used to restoring Clay's confidence. He'd done it in London with Cooper. Now he said: 'This is the big one, Daddy-o. Get off your ass, get back into that goddamned ring, and FIGHT!' He shoved Clay off the stool and back in to Liston. At the end of this round Liston flopped on his stool, burst into tears, complained of a hurt shoulder and relinquished the Richest Prize in Sport into Clay's care.

The new champion catapulted himself around the ring like a lunatic, screaming: 'I am the king! I am The Greatest! I told you all I'd whup Liston. I told you so. None of you believed me. But I did it. Oh, man, I am The Greatest!'

Did someone smear Liston's gloves with irritant? Was he really

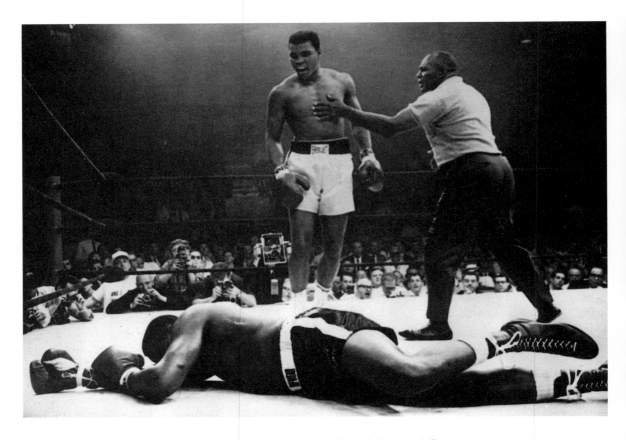

hurt enough to give up the heavyweight championship of the world? What the hell *was* going on? I don't know to this day. Inquiries were held. Liston's injury was diagnosed as bursitis, but no champion from the days of John L. Sullivan had ever sat down crying in the middle of a fight and surrendered because his shoulder hurt.

Their second fight, the following year, made even less sense. It took place in a school hockey arena in a rundown New England mill town called Lewiston, Maine, in front of 2,434 people. It went there because no normal boxing venue wanted to stage it after the Florida fiasco. They were right.

Halfway through round one Clay – sorry, Ali (he announced his Muslim allegiance immediately after the Miami shambles) – tossed an innocent-looking right hand which grazed Liston's temple. Sonny fell backwards and hit the floor with a crash. Ali stood over him, lips curled, brandishing a threatening fist. Frank Sinatra took a snapshot at this point. The picture is so dramatically good I used it on the dustjacket of a book I wrote. But the question has to be asked: what

Muhammad Ali's second win over Sonny Liston, Lewiston, Maine, 1965. The picture is ablaze with drama, but the scene deteriorated into farce. Jersey Joe Walcott, the referee, couldn't hear the count. Liston got up and fought back. Just when it was getting interesting again, they decided Liston had been knocked out after all. It all happened inside two minutes.

was big bad Sonny Liston doing lying on his back after taking a patsy punch to the side of the head?

I daresay Jersey Joe Walcott, the referee, was asking himself the same thing. He started counting and eventually Liston hauled himself off the floor and started fighting back. They were now having a serious battle.

Meanwhile, Nat Fleischer (the same Fleischer who had wised me up to Clay's existence), sitting next to the timekeeper, leapt to his feet, hammered his fist on the ring apron and yelled to Walcott: 'Stop the fight! Liston was counted out! Stop the fight!' Hearing Nat's bellow above the din, Walcott jumped between the two men, pulled Liston away, sent him to his corner and raised Clay's arm.

Fleischer explained he had been looking at the timekeeper's watch while Liston was down and seen it tick off 10 seconds before Liston got up. He had taken it on himself to raise the alarm, he said, because the timekeeper was a very elderly gentleman. Nat at this time was well into his eighties.

The ludicrous events of the evening were further compounded when the official time of the KO was given as 60 seconds, making it the second fastest heavyweight title finish of all time. I always hold a stopwatch on fights and I knew this couldn't be right. My watch, stopped at the point where Walcott intervened, read something like 1min 45sec, so the KO would have come round the 1min 30sec mark. Today the records say that Liston went down at 1min 42sec and that Walcott stopped it 30 seconds later, which puts the actual KO point at 1min 52sec. I still don't believe it.

Questioned about the right hand which sent Liston toppling, Ali rhapsodised about his new-found 'anchor' punch, which he said had been invented and handed on by Sam Langford, the Boston Tar Baby, who died blind and penniless, close to seventy years old, in 1956, when Ali was just fourteen.

I find it impossible to explain either of the Liston-Ali fights in logical terms. Undeniably, they changed the course of boxing history and many of its major assumptions. Ali was right when he caricatured heavyweights of old. Not even the best of them performed as he did. No big man had ever danced like a lightweight. Boxing experts found it nigh impossible to admit that successful heavyweight assault could be founded on fleeting feet. Over the next few years he proved them wrong and in so doing changed our conception of what a heavyweight champion should look like. For that reason alone Muhammad Ali is a seminal figure in boxing's history.

Like Sugar Ray Robinson before him, Ali maintained an expensive

Left *I took this in Miami in 1964 . . . that's Ali's first wife Sonji with him in the pink Cadillac. They had been married only a few months. It lasted less than a year.*

Below *Outside Ali's Miami bungalow. The minders are his Muslim colleagues. He had only recently joined the sect.*

retinue of camp servants. Some of the Muslim minders I never identified. They were never introduced. There was Sam Saxon, otherwise known as Cap'n Sam, Ali's principal bodyguard. I don't recall that he ever spoke to me. I suspect he looked on me as another white intruder who needed watching.

Angelo Dundee, the outstanding trainer of his time, was the one white man who had *carte blanche*. A passionate devotee of country-and-western music and an expert square dancer, Angelo was my greatest ally. Cap'n Sam could protest all he liked, but if Angelo whispered in Ali's ear that I needed to talk to him, the way was clear.

No one understood Ali as well as Angelo. He once explained the secret of handling him: 'If I want him to box, I tell him to fight. If I want him to rest, I tell him to keep busy. He just does every goddamn thing the reverse of what I tell him.'

Luis Sarria, a slim, slight Cuban, massaged the aches and pains out of Ali's magnificent frame, year in, year out. Luis didn't speak English. I'm not sure he spoke at all. I never heard him utter a single word all the years I watched him at work.

Finally, there was Bundini. Don't ask me why, but it was pronounced Bo-dini. His given name was Drew Brown and he was an adventurer. An ex-merchant seaman, he had been round the world and, having met Ali in 1963, just before the Doug Jones fight, mesmerised him with his sharp mind and corny philosophy. Bundini had read a lot in his lonely bunk at sea and when he'd had a couple of drinks he liked to discuss the larger issues, such as why are we here on earth and is God black or white? From the moment they met, they hit it off. He became Ali's closest companion and, eventually, a cornerman, to Angelo's dismay. Most of the advice Bundini bellowed at Ali was in direct contrast to what Dundee was trying to convey. Bundini, however, can claim a small share of immortality in boxing. Ali's early fame was built around the line: 'Float like a butterfly, sting like a bee.' Bundini invented that.

In between the two fights with Liston, BBC producer Les Kettley and I made an hour-long documentary on Ali for BBC-1. We spent three weeks in the States, commuting between Louisville, his birthplace, and Miami, where he lived with his first wife Sonji.

We parked on his doorstep for days on end, but were never permitted beyond it. Now and then Ali would flourish a copy of a Black Muslim newspaper under our noses and point out lurid cartoons in which 'white devils' roasted over everlasting flames. I don't think he regarded us as devils. Contempt was reserved for white Americans, or rednecks as he called them.

Exactly where he always wanted to be . . . in the spotlight. An impromptu interview on the Stardust Hotel stage in Las Vegas, during the run-up to the Floyd Patterson fight of 1965.

One day he came back from town with a big box under his arm. He had bought a croquet set and asked me if I'd heard of the game. I explained it was a royal and ancient game that had been played in England for centuries. We wound up knocking balls through hoops on a grassy traffic island in the middle of the nearest highway.

With filming complete, we went to the Fifth Street gym in Miami Beach where he trained (and where he once persuaded all four Beatles to lie on the floor in the ring while he planted a regal foot on them; they loved it). Les and I thanked him for his help in making the documentary. He laughed and said: 'Whaddya gonna pay me then?'

Les went through his impeccable 'you know how hard up the Beeb is' routine and convinced Ali no payment was forthcoming. 'Hey,

So why am I standing on a box on the sidewalk in Glendale, a Los Angeles suburb? That big guy on the right is Primo Carnera, one-time heavyweight champion, and he's close to 6ft 7in tall. We're outside his liquor store and I am interviewing him for a TV series called The Richest Prize in Sport. *Bob Duncan, BBC producer, in the middle, said I'd look ridiculous without the box. I sure as hell look ridiculous with* it.

man,' protested Ali, 'I need money, honey, to buy Cokes and things. What you got in your pocket?'

Les dug into his trousers and came up with a crumpled twenty-dollar bill. 'That's all I have, honest,' wailed Les.

'That'll do,' said Ali and snatched it out of Les's hand. An hour-long Muhammad Ali spectacular, and the star settles for twenty bucks. Mickey Duff would have been proud of us.

After Lewiston, Ali steadily wiped out all doubts about his ability by taking on allcomers. He packed eight title defences into the next two years, beating Floyd Patterson, George Chuvalo, Henry Cooper (again), Brian London, Karl Mildenberger, Cleveland Williams, Ernie Terrell and Zora Folley. As win followed win, he dispersed criticism of his style, convincing even his toughest critics he was something special: a worthy world champion and a supreme showman.

Boxing now loved him . . . until, in 1967, when called on to register for national service, he refused to swear the oath of allegiance to the US flag. America was embroiled in the bitter Vietnam war. Ali found simple words to explain where he stood as a Muslim: 'I ain't got no argument with them Viet Cong.'

Every boxing association in the world stripped him of his title. He was sentenced to five years in jail and fined 10,000 dollars. While his lawyers appealed, Ali was banished from the scene and lesser men scrambled for the spoils.

In 1968, when Bob Duncan and I were making *The Richest Prize in Sport*, a history of the world heavyweight championship, we tracked Ali down to a seedy motel on Segundo Boulevard in a suburb of Los Angeles. He was the final chapter of a seven-part series that went back to the days of John L. Sullivan. He sat on his bed and we talked of where events had brought him. I had just one more question to put to close the series. 'Ali,' I said, 'surely you must miss boxing?'

'No, Harry,' he said softly, and found the right, simple words again. 'Boxing misses me.'

7

A New Set of Friends

If a letter shaped my life in 1948, a phone call added a new dimension to it in 1965. On the line from Manchester, where he was BBC-TV's Senior Sports Producer, was Ray Lakeland, a genial, no-nonsense Northerner with whom I'd shared many a boxing commentary and pint.

'Fancy doing a bit of golf, then?' asked Ray. I thought he might be pulling my leg. He had an impish humour. In those last few moments before you go on the air, when the tension fairly crackles, Ray had a way of defusing it by gently murmuring down your headphones: 'Shall we stand ever so slightly by?' But he was serious: 'Cliff Michelmore, my link-man on golf, has moved on to bigger and better things. Do you want to take his place?'

It was a serious question which needed some thought. I mulled it over for all of three seconds before saying, 'Yes, please.' I fronted BBC's golf for the next quarter of a century.

Sitting ringside at boxing has been the major part of my life for nearly half a century and people ask the simple question: why? I don't find it hard to answer.

Boxing is about man himself, about survival, about life. The veneer of what we call civilisation is thin indeed (watch what happens on the garage forecourt when petrol is short). Life remains a tough business and to get through it without stepping outside the law requires self-discipline and courage.

Boxing demonstrates these qualities vividly. It is also dependent, no matter what its critics may think, on considerable technique. Boxing is the basic sport, man to man, no weapons other than your own fists and skill. My admiration for boxers is boundless. Usually at ringside I am either flushed with excitement or racked with anxiety. It is, and always will be, dangerous. So is life.

Is it strange that I should have married the coverage of boxing for twenty-five years with that of golf? The will to win is about all they have in common. And yet I never found it difficult to step from one to the other (apart from the time when I returned from golf to boxing and described a close round as halved).

Golf also teaches us a few lessons about how to behave in life. Henry Longhurst talked of it as 'taking you to beautiful places'. What I enjoyed above that was the quiet dignity of the game, the essential *slowness* of it, the immaculate turnout of the competitors, the absence of cheating and histrionics, and the controlled excitement of the spectators, most of whom play the game and understand it.

I relished the change of pace from the instant, crashing excitement of a championship fight, which comes and goes within the hour, to the relentless, increasing pressure of a golf championship, which builds to its climax over four days.

The BBC golf team of bygone days. Left to right: *Bruce Critchley, debonair Old Etonian; Clive Clark, ex-Walker and Ryder Cup star who came close to winning the Open at Hoylake in 1967; Peter Alliss, winner of umpteen tournaments and now the world's top golfing commentator; Alex Hay, the livewire Scot who runs the immaculate Woburn Club; and finally the only one among them who can't play the game very well.*

Right *At home in Dulwich, with my wife and son, honing my game to its usual level of mediocrity.*

I can claim a Wentworth championship myself. David Coleman and I won the GRA Foursomes there in the 1960s. Laddie Lucas, ex-Walker Cup player and GRA Chairman, handed over our prize: a car-rug apiece. The success never went to my head . . . and was never repeated.

Four days! Do I have to explain the heady thrill of fronting a TV event which keeps the nation glued to its screens for four days? Or the even more seductive charms of Wimbledon, where you remorselessly confront the viewer on both BBC channels for a fortnight?

I watched twenty-five Open Championships, from Nicklaus at Muirfield to Faldo at St Andrews. I shall never be short of memories . . . of Nicklaus stripping off his sweater on the 18th at St Andrews in the 1978 Open and ripping the ball all the way to the pin (354 yards) and beyond it. It rolled on and on, coming to rest only a foot or two short of the out-of-bounds at the back of the green . . .

. . . of little Mr Lu, from Formosa, gently doffing his pork-pie hat to the cheering crowds at Birkdale in 1971, losing by a mere stroke to Trevino . . .

. . . of nineteen-year-old Ballesteros bursting on the scene, again at Birkdale, in 1976, tying second with Nicklaus behind Johnny Miller . . . and playing out of the car park at the 17th, Royal Lytham, 1979, to win his first Open . . .

. . . and of Tom Watson, winning his five Opens, from 1975 to 1983. We started calling our interview at the 18th on the final day our 'annual meeting'.

Right Never was there such a confrontation . . . Jack Nicklaus and Tom Watson played head-to-head, shot-for-shot, over the final two days of the 1977 Turnberry Open. Watson won by a single stroke with a record score. Jack graciously gave way to a better man on the day.

*

Watson was involved in the finest Open I ever saw: the head-to-head battle with Nicklaus at Turnberry in 1977. Watson was twenty-seven, Nicklaus ten years older.

The amazing moments at the end of the final round are always recalled, but it is sometimes forgotten that the two men also played head-to-head in the previous round. Both went round the Ailsa course in 65 and their scores after three rounds were identical.

On the final day Nicklaus went three strokes ahead after four holes. But, as they teed up at the 15th, Watson was only one behind. At this par-3 hole Watson put his tee shot ten feet off the green to the left. Nicklaus was on the putting surface, Watson sixty feet from the pin. Jack later confessed: 'I thought he'd be lucky to get down in two.'

Watson took his putter on the hard ground, the ball hit the flagstick and dropped in. They were level with three to play. On the par-5 17th (Lang Whang), Watson got there with a drive and a three-iron. Nicklaus chose a four-iron, left it short, and took three more. Watson two-putted for his birdie. For the first time that day, Tom was ahead.

Sensibly he drew the one-iron from his bag at the 18th and lashed the ball down the middle. Nicklaus, needing a birdie to tie, smashed with his driver and sent the ball out to the right, well nigh unplayable under a gorse bush.

While Jack pondered, Tom hit a seven-iron that rolled up two feet from the hole. All Jack could do was slash with an eight-iron. The ball came to rest just off the green, thirty-odd feet from the pin. I was kneeling there, waiting to interview the winner, when Jack putted the ball into the hole! It was one of the most courageous and defiant acts in the history of golf. Watson quickly walked to his ball and tapped it in before the challenge Jack had thrown down sank in. Watson's 268 was eight strokes better than any previous winner's. He and Jack are the only men to beat 270 in the Open.

That heroic battle had all the ingredients of a heavyweight boxing championship, without the physical pain. Perhaps the difference between the sports is not so enormous after all.

Having earlier praised the disciplined behaviour of golfing galleries, I should add a note of warning. Welcome as Britain and Europe's late-found success in the Ryder Cup may be, the attitude of some spectators is far from welcome. At the Belfry in 1985 and again in 1989 there was an overlay of chauvinism which led to raucous cheering (and jeering) when an American golfer found trouble. It reeks of the mindless fan worship which disfigures soccer and, increasingly, boxing. It is so out of keeping with golf I find it obscene.

I noted a remark by Dave Stockton, the US team manager, at the

Now there was a pleasure and a privilege . . . to work alongside the one and only Henry Longhurst. That umbrella is there either (a) to shield the monitor-screens from the sun's glare, or (b) to protect them from rain coming through the studio roof. The latter is more likely.

1991 Ryder Cup in South Carolina. He said the event was in danger of becoming 'a war'. That is true of so much sport today. Sport was meant to be something you did basically for your own enjoyment. Misplaced national pride and massive prize money have turned it into something else.

Lakeland's offer widened my career, gave me a new set of friends and turned working into sheer pleasure. It was late summer when Ray phoned. My first assignments included the Ryder Cup at Royal Birkdale and the Piccadilly World Matchplay at Wentworth.

Peter Alliss was in the British Ryder Cup team. I didn't know then how much enjoyable work we'd get through together in the BBC commentary box. He was still a front-line player. I see from my old programme that, with Christy O'Connor, he won three of his four 'doubles' matches at Birkdale and then went on to win both his singles, against Billy Casper and Ken Venturi. It accounted for almost half of Great Britain's points. Arnold Palmer didn't do as well for America.

As the years went by the commentator's accommodation on the golf course became ever more luxurious. When I said goodbye in 1990 we were housed in a huge purpose-built studio with carpet on the floor, comfortable armchairs, Venetian blinds to shield our eyes from the sun, and Lionel and Betty sustaining us through the long day with cups of coffee and chocolate biscuits. It was different in those early days with Ray.

There was no studio. Commentators sat out in the open on the camera platforms, exposed to the elements. If it rained a kindly stage manager such as Harry Coventry, Bob Clarkson or Mike Huffleman would stand guard over you with an umbrella. Less benign ones – such gentlemen do exist – would make sure the rain dripped steadily off the umbrella down the back of your neck.

In October 1965, I was perched on the camera scaffolding overlooking the 15th green and 16th tee on the West Course at Wentworth, where Arnold Palmer was defending his World Matchplay title. I sat at a small fold-up card table with Bill Cox, the commentator, and a scorer who manned the giant sheet which logs progress of the matches. Apart from linking in and out of items, it was my job to keep up with the scores and tip Bill off to any interesting developments.

As Palmer marched towards the green where he'd laid his approach shot, I spotted something interesting. I scribbled a hasty note on a small piece of paper and passed it to Bill. Well, almost. As I went to put it in front of him a swirling wind caught it, lifted it over the scaffolding rail, from where it floated down to come to rest on the 15th green, which Palmer had now reached. Arnie strode straight towards the offending scrap of paper, picked it up, and read it.

I had written: 'Palmer has three-putted the last three greens.'

He stuffed it in his pocket, lined up a twenty-foot putt and sank it. I understood then what makes the Palmers of this world so good at their job.

In 1966 I covered my first Open, at Muirfield on the eastern shores of Scotland where Jack Nicklaus needed a par-4 at the final

Right No one had a follow-through like Arnold Palmer. He won the inaugural World Matchplay Championship at Wentworth in 1964 . . . and a few other things as well.

hole to beat Dave Thomas of Wales and Doug Sanders of America. He got it, of course, with a one-iron, three-iron and two putts, to win his first Open and a prize of £1,750.

Like the prize money then and now, Jack then bore little resemblance to Jack now. His hair was cropped short and he was podgy. Media protocol at the end of the Open in those days was different, too. The Royal and Ancient today lays down a scrupulous timetable from the moment the winner taps in his final putt. He steps into the recorder's hut, checks and signs his card, then moves out to the fringes of the 18th green where the presentation ceremony takes place. He is ushered to the BBC interviewer and the ensuing chat is relayed to the crowds surrounding the final green.

It wasn't like that in '66. If we wanted Nicklaus we had to find him and persuade him to talk to us. When I say 'we' I mean Slim Wilkinson, the BBC-TV producer, who eventually took over from Lakeland as our golfing supremo. Slim found Jack and brought him to the interview position. You've guessed it: up on the camera platform and reachable only by a vertical ladder lashed to the scaffolding. Jack took one look at the situation and said firmly: 'I don't like ladders.'

'But we want you to talk to Harry,' said Slim.

'Who's Harry?' asked Jack.

Slim must have been honey-tongued because the next thing I saw, as I peered over the rail, was Nicklaus on his way up the ladder. Then I saw the way he was coming up. Slim was two rungs below with two hands shoving Jack's ample backside, I suppose in case he changed his mind halfway up. Those were the days.

Nicklaus was not alone in his hatred of those daunting ladders. Henry Longhurst was physically incapable of climbing them and, when he first went to the States to do the Masters, told the Americans so in no uncertain fashion. They went away and designed a splendid staircase with wide steps – which the BBC also adopted – and to this day the steps that lead to any US commentary box are known as the Longhurst Ladder, a nice way to keep the old boy's name alive across the Atlantic. Not that Henry needs any help; he made his own legends.

What a privilege it was to have worked alongside Henry *Carpenter* Longhurst (you can imagine the pleasure that middle name gave me). I did so for well over ten years. He was a mine of wit and wisdom, a man whose philosophy was to try everything once. He had been a deep-sea diver, driven a train and hurtled down the Cresta Run. He had also been an MP.

He described how he had once driven through West London in a

Left *The first Open I covered for BBC Television: Jack Nicklaus's win at Muirfield, 1966. He was resented by US fans at first, because he threatened Arnold Palmer's supremacy. He reshaped his public image by losing weight and letting his hair grow. The Golden Bear was born. There will be no greater golfer than Nicklaus in my time.*

hired car with Arnold Palmer. When they reached Acton, Henry casually mentioned it had once been his constituency. Palmer was astonished to discover that Henry, in 1943, had been declared the Conservative member.

'Yes,' said Henry. 'It may be a long time ago, but I can recall as if it were yesterday standing on those very steps [they were now passing the Central Hall] after the votes had been counted and telling the assembled throng what I stood for and how I intended to do my best for them in the Mother of Parliaments.'

'Really?' said the fascinated Palmer. 'And what was their reaction?'

'They just stood there muttering bollocks,' said Henry.

He had a sharp eye for affectation and I was a victim. In 1968 BBC Television went into colour and frontmen like myself thought we should rise to the challenge. I began wearing very gaudy, striped ties. One day as we were leaving the commentary box Henry laid a gentle hand on my arm and said: 'Now, Harry, I've been looking with some interest at that tie you're wearing. You must tell me. Are those your old school colours or your own unfortunate choice?' The tie was never seen again.

No British golfer had won the Open since Max Faulkner in 1951. A year or two after I started, the name of Tony Jacklin, a former Assistants' champion from Potters Bar, began popping up. His hole in one with a seven-iron at the 163-yard 16th at Royal St George's in the 1967 Dunlop Masters was the first seen on TV. He had a knack of making news. I remember a shot – was it in the Viyella tournament at Wentworth? – that hit the green at a par-3, took a bounce, and disappeared. A woman sitting by the green showed her open handbag. The ball was in it.

Then came 1969. I can see him now in the lilac sweater, wearing just one shoe (the other was wrenched off while he was pushing through the cheering mob), walking towards me off the 18th at Royal Lytham, throwing his arms round Vivien, who was carrying their first child, then telling me what it was like to be Britain's first Open champion for eighteen years. It was the most joyous interview I have ever had.

Jacklin now had the golden touch. Less than a year after Lytham, he won the 1970 US Open at Hazeltine by seven strokes, so that when he came to St Andrews for the Open he was champion golfer on both sides of the Atlantic. The magic continued. In his opening round, he birdied holes one, two, three, five and seven, and then, at the par-4 9th, hit a wedge from 100 yards that went in. He was out in 29, seven under par. He birdied the 10th, had pars at the 11th, 12th and

Britain celebrated Tony Jacklin's Open Championship at Royal Lytham, 1969, with good reason. He was the first British winner for nearly twenty years.

13th, and left his second at the 14th under a gorse bush, his first mistake. At this point, an almighty thunderstorm and cloudburst flooded the Old Course and sent every competitor scurrying for cover. Tony had to come back shortly after dawn the next morning. Not surprisingly, the magic had evaporated. He finished with a 67. It could easily have been a 62.

In 1972 at the Muirfield Open Jacklin came to the par-5 17th on the final day tied for the lead with Lee Trevino, his playing partner. The BBC commentary box overlooked the 17th green. I saw what happened from the moment they teed off. Tony hit two good woods and was just short of the green. Lee hooked his drive into a bunker, played out sideways, hit his third into the left rough and his fourth way up on the bank at the back of the green in none too good a lie. Tony had three for his par. Lee would be lucky to get a six.

Tony chipped up on to a green heavily marked after four days' play. The ball stopped some fifteen feet short, but he was still the master of the situation. My distinct impression at the time was that Trevino had had enough. He took no time or care about the chip. He made a stab at the ball, it scuttled down the bank . . . and went in. Five! Tony's putt, his fourth shot, went well past, and he missed the one back. Trevino won the Open. Jacklin didn't even finish second.

I remember Henry Longhurst commenting at the time that Jacklin was too great a golfer not to come back and win at least one more Open. He never did. What Trevino did to him that day stayed with him through the rest of his career. He was like a boxer who had been badly hurt in a fight and could never forget it.

Some critics hammered Jacklin hard for not winning everything in sight over the next few years. That was too harsh. Jacklin won 'ours and theirs' at a time when British golf was at its lowest ebb. His magic alone put the spark to the great fire of European achievement which engulfed the Americans in the 1980s.

Only when you stand off and look back do you appreciate the awesome ability of certain men and women. In golf I have lived and worked through the age of Nicklaus supremacy: twenty major titles, never remotely approached by any other person. In a hundred years' time Nicklaus will be seen as a godlike figure bestriding all others.

Left *The police escort is impressive. Was it for Tony . . . or the trophy? His superb win at Lytham paved the way for British and European success which eventually swept the Americans aside.*

8

Dead Men's Shoes

There's a touch of 'dead men's shoes' in my business. You pick up jobs that others drop. That's how I came to be the frontman at Wimbledon. David Coleman did it for years, then one day – God bless you, David – decided he could do without it. In 1967 I was handed the Wimbledon job.

Newcombe, Rosewall, Emerson and Roche . . . Bueno, Court, King and Jones . . . these were the big names in my early days. In the men's singles we moved on to Smith, Connors, Ashe, Borg, McEnroe, Becker and Edberg. In the women's came Evert, Goolagong, Navratilova and Graf. I feel very lucky to have worked alongside such huge stars of the game. Nothing can ever take away the enjoyment of being able to say I was there when Ann Jones won for Britain in 1969, and when Virginia Wade won in 1977, not only putting the ultimate gloss on Wimbledon's centenary year, but also being clever enough to arrange her peak form when The Queen was paying one of her rare visits to the supreme stage of lawn tennis.

As the BBC years have worn on, I cannot deny the thrill of fronting an event where these two ladies commentate, where I can go into the TV interview room and talk to Martina Navratilova, the greatest woman tennis player of my time, or chat to Billie-Jean King, whose grasp of media technique is second to none. These are heady pleasures and I am not ashamed to admit being seduced by them.

Getting the Wimbledon job was the consummation of a lifetime's love for the sport. Just as I had crouched by the wireless as a boy to

Top left *Stan Smith, tall and soldierly: his Sunday final with Nastase, 1972, was a classic.*

Top right *Ilie Nastase, touch-player par excellence. A comedy routine degenerated into vulgarity.*

Jimmy Connors, Wimbledon champion twice, runner-up four times. Unsubtle humour never eroded his popularity with the crowd.

Bjorn Borg, the finest men's champion of my Wimbledon years. His record may never be equalled.

listen to the big fights, so I had spent long, hot summer afternoons in the 1930s absorbing BBC Radio commentaries from Wimbledon.

Even now, I can remember matches involving Fred Perry, Bunny Austin and Don Budge. One Friday afternoon in 1937, in my aunt's house in Croydon, I listened to Dorothy Round, a Sunday school teacher from Worcestershire, winning the Wimbledon final against her Polish opponent, Jadwiga Jedrzejowska. The obvious impossibility of getting his tongue round the Polish girl's name in every rally led the commentator (it may well have been Freddie Grisewood) to call her 'Jed'. I wonder if he had his knuckles rapped by the authoritarian John Reith, the BBC's first Director General?

In 1977, I sat in the Wimbledon players' lounge and interviewed Dorothy Round, exactly forty years on from that Friday afternoon in front of the wireless. Experiences like this confirm life's weird and wonderful ways.

Dorothy Round, or Mrs Little as she became, was a few days short of her sixty-eighth birthday when we talked. She had won Wimbledon twice in the 1930s, but her modesty was such that she seemed almost too embarrassed to mention it. It's a pity some modern players, with far less to their credit, are not as reticent.

Right John McEnroe, mighty talent undermined by unruly temperament. Obscenity on court is unforgivable.

Left *Boris Becker, teenage wunderkind.*

Stefan Edberg, temperamental Swede. On his day, no one better.

Ann Jones, Britain's first women's champion since Angela Mortimer. She had to beat Billie-Jean in the '69 final.

Perhaps the pace of modern life – and the demands of the media – force competitors into a brash, glib way of looking at their achievements. In my early days in Fleet Street it was rare for sports columnists to seek 'quotes' from players. Journalists gave *their* opinion on what they had seen. Now it is required practice for sports writers to grab the 'nannies' (nanny-goats: quotes). Indeed, in tennis and other big-money sports, competitors are compelled under their contracts to give post-match interviews to TV, radio and the Press.

It is hardly surprising that most of the 'quotes' are worthless. Competitors say precisely what you expect them to say. Thirty or forty years ago, if you felt someone had something worth saying, you worked hard to get him or her to talk to you . . . exclusively. If a rival newspaperman nosed his way in, you had wasted your time.

How many times have I climbed through the ropes at the end of a fight and thrust a microphone under the winner's nose? And how many times has it produced anything really worth hearing?

I am not saying that competitors' thoughts on their work have no value. Delivered at the right moment under the right conditions they can be extremely revealing. But our – the media's – insane thirst for quotes round the clock has devalued the product.

Right Billie-Jean King, most successful player ever at Wimbledon, with twenty titles, six of them in the singles. Off court she revitalised the administration of women's tennis.

People rightly say: 'I'd love to have your job, travelling the world, meeting all the great stars of sport, and watching them for nothing.' True, it's a good life, but somewhere along the line you have to pay for everything you get. The people who would 'love your job' would probably not enjoy the drudgery behind the scenes, the hours and hours spent entering up boxing results on index cards, cutting and filing newspaper reports on every sport, researching and preparing notes on the events you cover. I'm not complaining. I'm just saying there's a lot more to it than just sitting in the commentary box.

Wimbledon happens to be the one job where I collect sympathy. It has not been forgotten that for years I introduced Wimbledon from underground, spending the fortnight in a 'bunker' below No. 1 Court, emerging into daylight only when the call of nature demanded it. The bunker was my middle period.

My first 'home' at Wimbledon was a giant green shed, almost the size of an aeroplane hangar, built each year in Barker's Field. In hot summers it was a nightmare: no air-conditioning, just a couple of lazy fans swirling the foetid air about. Outside, we had a small garden. Well, it looked like a garden. Actually, it was a stretch of white trellis-work with artificial climbing plants, a few garden chairs and a

Above left Virginia Wade . . . *a dish to set before The Queen in 1977.*

Above right Graceful and modest with it: Evonne Cawley, née Goolagong.

Right Chris Evert, ever-popular. She won with style, lost with grace. Chrissie played in ten singles finals at Wimbledon.

white wrought-iron table. Dan Maskell, Peter West, Jack Kramer and I used to sit there chatting about the day's tennis. It had a distinct Wimbledon 'feel' and whoever designed it should have been congratulated, but certainly never was.

Then I was moved down to the bunker, never as bad as its reputation. It was restricted for space, certainly, although I had a large desk, seven or eight monitor sets, and the company of the caption people, i.e. John Tidy, Andy Bloomfield and several others, all of whom were cheerful company and kept me sane.

The bunker's one great advantage over the terrible green shed was its air-conditioning. Here was a cool, quiet place to work and, furthermore, it was right alongside the control room. I could stroll from my desk to the heart of the operation in just a few paces. It's no bad thing to be that close to the clockwork.

The bunker was OK, but the embarrassment of coming up like a mole into the daylight, running slap into the queues of spectators waiting to enter the two main showcourts, and have them see you sprinting smartly into the gent's lavatory was irksome. That's where I deserved the sympathy. My toilet strategy was public knowledge for years.

Above left *Martina Navratilova, unquestionably the greatest woman player of all time. Her ninth Wimbledon win in 1990 knocked Helen Wills-Moody's record out of the books.*

Above right *Steffi Graf . . . she and Becker cleaned up Wimbledon's singles for Germany in 1989. She did it again with Michael Stich in '91.*

Those early TV days at Wimbledon . . . the 'garden patio' where Dan Maskell, Jack Kramer, Peter West and I would look forward to the day's play. It was rigged up by the scene-shifters. The flowers were phoney. But it looked right and I was sorry when we abandoned it.

When Barker's Field was turned into additional courts (No. 14 and upwards), the Beeb built a palatial new studio overlooking Court 14. My desk became bigger still, more and more monitors were added, and I had switches to hand that controlled sound and vision. I lost the company of the caption mob. They stayed downstairs in the bunker. Now I had my own make-up cubicle and my own make-up girl. Traitor that I am, I must admit her company was often more appealing than that of John Tidy and Co.

As the studio has a vast picture window (one-way vision) that looks out on to Court 14 where many important matches are played, well-meaning folk said: 'What a relief for you after that terrible place underground. Now you can watch some tennis.' I hate to disillusion them. I sat at the Wimbledon desk with my back to the window. I saw about as much tennis up there as I did down below.

In 1972 there was a men's final so good that Dan Maskell still refers to it as one of the best he has seen. Stan Smith, a tall, soldierly American, overcame Ilie Nastase of Romania in five glorious sets. Smith's power just had the edge on Nastase's finesse. This match was the zenith of Nastase's mercurial career. His early days, when

BBC's Wimbledon commentary team, 1971. Dan Maskell, of course, and with him America's Jack Kramer, who won Wimbledon in 1947, and pipe-smoking Peter West, one of the best and most versatile commentators we ever had.

he mixed artistic tennis with gentle clowning, were a joy to watch. I never saw a player with as much flair and touch. Unhappily, as his wealth increased, the discipline fell from his game, the comedy stuff became grotesque and eventually turned into abuse of officials. A talent that should have flowered simply withered.

Nastase and Jimmy Connors, whose humour on court frequently spilled over into four-letter obscenity, were the forerunners of John McEnroe, a player who should have been severely and properly dealt with in his younger days. There is something inherently wrong with a sport that permits McEnroe, a genius with the racket and a menace with his mouth, to insult officials and disturb opponents with behaviour that, if perpetrated in the streets, could have led to an appearance in court.

I understand exactly why he was allowed to get away with it. Sponsors paying huge money to back a tournament don't want their star player pulled out. McEnroe was a box-office winner, despite – or perhaps because of – his appalling reputation. I cannot respect an attitude that favours expediency above common decency. McEnroe's behaviour was unforgivable and had no place in something calling itself sport.

Right A scene that became all too familiar: the accusing finger directed at the net-cord judge, the reproving gesture from the umpire.

Fortunately, Bjorn Borg's teenage tantrums died out and a fierce concentration on the job in hand took their place, allowing him the almost unbelievable sequence of five Wimbledon wins, plus a narrow defeat by McEnroe in his sixth successive final. As a man at Wimbledon must win seven consecutive matches to take the championship, Borg ran up a sequence of forty-one wins before McEnroe beat him. Given the depth of talent in tennis, Borg's feat ranks among the immortal achievements at Wimbledon.

And yet, in 1990, a full ten years after his last Wimbledon title, I was on my way to a fight in Italy when I bumped into Bjorn at Milan Airport. He was trying to make a comeback. He was clearly miserable and I wondered why a man who had achieved so much should still be chasing fulfilment at a time when his talent had deserted him. He made me feel sad and apprehensive. If success like Borg's leads to despondency, what hope is there for the rest of us? Professional sport has a lot to answer for.

Alongside Borg's supremacy at Wimbledon must go Martina Navratilova's record in an era which included Chris Evert and Steffi Graf. I doubt if the onlooker can really understand the burning thirst of ambition which drives a woman like Martina to her goal, the eclipse of Helen Wills-Moody's record of eight titles. She won nine and appeared in eleven of the thirteen finals between 1978 and 1990. It was a privilege to front Wimbledon for the BBC during these amazing years.

9

The Triumvirate

In boxing Joe Louis remains the supreme champion. I wish I had seen him fight. Here was a man who reeled off twenty-five successful defences of the world heavyweight crown, either side of World War II. By the time I got to know him, he was scraping a living on the publicity staff at Muhammad Ali's fights. It is all very well to say that some professional sportsmen and women can't cope with the problems of being exceptional champions. Surely the sport itself has the responsibility of seeing that the people it rewards can handle the problems?

Ali is the outstanding heavyweight of my time. He might possibly have challenged Louis's record. In his first three years as champion he defended the title nine times, but his confrontation with American patriotism halted him. Ironically, the US public eventually came down on Ali's side in abhorrence of the Vietnam slaughter. Although he never went to jail or paid his fine, his punishment in boxing terms was bad enough: more than three years in exile. He was twenty-five when the ban came down, twenty-eight when it was lifted, of all places, in Georgia, once a hotbed of slavery. I flew to Atlanta in October 1970, to see him return in triumph with a three-round savaging of white contender Jerry Quarry.

That night in the Municipal Auditorium was a celebration of black affluence. Women were bedecked in fur and diamonds. Men flourished black velvet capes lined with red silk and sported floppy,

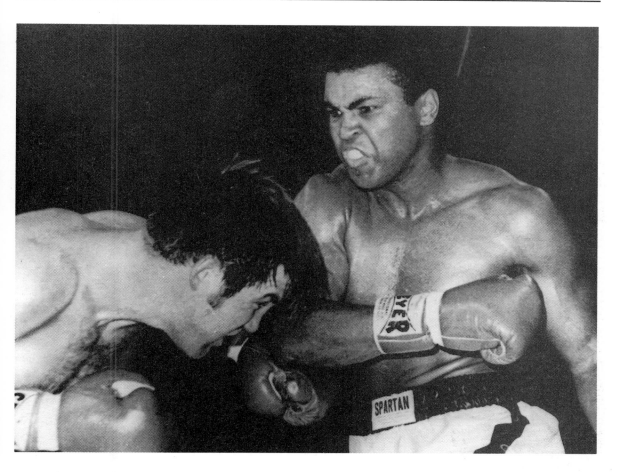

Muhammad Ali made short work of California's Jerry Quarry the night he was allowed to return to the ring in 1970. He was relicensed by the state of Georgia, once a hotbed of slavery.

Left *The man who'd been through it all: Joe Louis, heavyweight champion from 1937 to '49. Here in Las Vegas, 1965, he helped publicise the Ali-Patterson fight. Joe died, penniless, in 1981, aged sixty-six.*

broad-brimmed hats of beaver skin. Gold knuckleduster rings were jammed on every finger. These black millionaires were known as 'The Beautiful People' and Muhammad Ali was their god. He did not let them down on this night in Georgia, but when they returned to their mansions, many found their homes ransacked.

While Ali lay banished, Joe Frazier won his way to the title. Joe was the antithesis of his rival. Where Ali danced, Joe shuffled. Where Ali flashed a rapier, Joe wielded an axe. Where Ali dazzled with words, Joe mumbled threats. But Frazier was a great fighter, impervious to pain, a steamroller waiting to flatten you.

After one more comeback against Oscar Bonavena of Argentina, with Ali flogging Bonavena into submission in the fifteenth and final round, a multi-million dollar package was put together for a show-down with Frazier in New York City. Nothing like it had been attempted before. Each man would receive two-and-a-half million dollars, just over a million pounds apiece. Ringside seats cost 150 dollars, over 60 pounds. They sold for five times that on the night.

The fight was beamed into 350 theatres in the USA and Canada, into thirty-three in the UK. More than thirty countries took satellite transmissions. It was the first time two unbeaten fighters had met for the heavyweight championship. The world wanted to know if Ali was still The Greatest. No fancy label was needed to sell the promotion. They simply tagged it 'The Fight'.

Under a heavy veil of secrecy the BBC, through Peter Dimmock, Head of Outside Broadcasts, paid some colossal sum of money, buying the right to show the fight throughout Britain the following evening. Bob Duncan and I were despatched to the States to compile an hour-long preview, to be shown a few hours before the fight. No mention of this programme, or of The Fight itself, ever appeared in *Radio Times*.

Bob and I chased the two men over thousands of miles. Ali trained at his usual haunt, the Fifth Street gym in Miami Beach. Joe was in his native Philadelphia. He worked out on North Broad Street in an area which encapsulated all the things that were tough about Frazier. He wasn't exactly a Liston, but he had that same hard black ghetto shell. Joe made his own music on guitar and for a time led a rock-and-roll band. His greatest asset, other than his innate ferocity, was the father-figure of Yancey 'Yank' Durham, a railroad worker turned trainer-manager. Yank had a mature philosophical outlook which got through to Joe and tempered the wild man in him.

When other BBC people in London found out that Bob and I were working on The Fight, requests came thick and fast. I churned out pieces down the phone for radio and composed an entirely separate preview for *Sportsnight with Coleman*. The last straw, a day or two before The Fight, was a request from *Grandstand* for yet another preview. Outside the Fifth Street gym I stared at the camera and then at Duncan.

'Bob,' I said. 'I've had it. I'm dried up. I've said everything I can about this fight. There's nothing left.'

Duncan walked over, laid a hand on my shoulder, looked me in the eyes and sighed. 'Listen, sunshine,' he said quietly. 'Tell 'em where you are, tell 'em why you're here and tell 'em what you think's going to happen. Now get on with it.'

Simple, really. Just occasionally you need someone who can get you back to basics when the brain is reeling. Bob was good at that and I am eternally grateful to him for all the years he put up with me.

8 March 1971: the day of The Fight. New York City was near

Happy radio days working for producer Angus Mackay in his trail-blazing Saturday show, Sports Report. *For a long time I reviewed the week's sporting Press. It gave me a chance to have a dig at my old Fleet Street buddies, but cost me a small fortune in newspapers.*

hysteria over the most expensive single event in the history of sport. The two men were ordered to weigh-in ninety minutes apart to prevent a confrontation like the one Ali had had with Liston seven years before. Ali turned up an hour late. He couldn't get through the screaming mob outside his hotel, which was only a few blocks from Madison Square Garden, on Eighth Avenue.

As he neared the scales, publicity man John Condon announced him as 'the former heavyweight champion'. That set him off. 'Former champion?' he yelled. 'Tonight I'll show you who's the real champ. Frazier's ugly, clumsy, flat-footed. I'm the real champ.' He quietened down briefly while he weighed in at 15st 5lb, more than nine pounds heavier than Frazier. He began yelling again as his handlers led him back to the dressing-room. Ten minutes later, dressed in his outdoor clothes, he reappeared in the upper tiers of the arena, waving his arms and shouting down at the riggers who were assembling the ring: 'I'll be here tonight to show you who's the real champion of the world.'

I am way out of step with most people on this fight. There was a shattering climax when Frazier sent Ali sprawling with a busted jaw in the fifteenth round to put the result beyond doubt. But some rounds were strangely unreal, sessions of pit-a-pat punching, staccato taps that meant nothing. It didn't seem to me to live up to its

Ali crashes down in the fifteenth round of his 1971 fight with Joe Frazier in Madison Square Garden. Frazier kept his title. Ali suffered his first defeat, a damaged jaw and an almighty blow to his pride. It was the most expensive sports event ever staged . . . at the time.

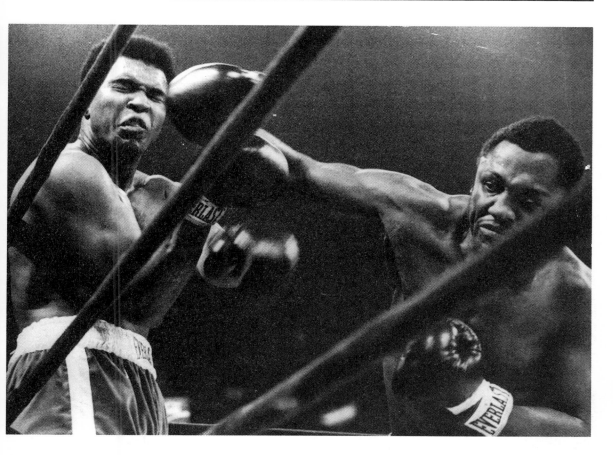

Although Frazier made this punch tell, Ali beat him over twelve rounds at Madison Square Garden in 1974. It was doubly important for Ali. He had revenge over Frazier and was now set to challenge Foreman for the title.

promise, although the result smashed Ali's claim to be the real champion. He actually admitted to Joe at the end, 'You're the champ.' Defeat sent him into the wilderness for another three years.

Within three hours of the finish, I was heading for London in a TWA freight plane which took off from JFK in a snowstorm at two o'clock in the morning. I carried with me the videotape of The Fight. From Heathrow the tape and I were rushed to Lime Grove and, a few hours after we landed, we were on the air. The secret mission was over.

The man who waved that tiny Stars and Stripes in Mexico City was now thrust forward as Frazier's most dangerous challenger. George Foreman, delinquent turned lay preacher, had an Oriental impassivity about him. He was no easy interview in his younger days. He liked to keep his German shepherd dog at his feet. I was never sure whether he called it Daggo or Doggo. Either way it was a menacing brute, and you could say much the same of George, as Frazier found out.

Almost two years after Ali's defeat, Frazier faced Foreman in Kingston, Jamaica, in another heavyweight title fight between unbeaten men. Within two rounds Foreman had battered Frazier to the floor six times, the final punch being one of the most dramatic I have seen. A right uppercut lifted Frazier off the floor. Both feet came off the canvas before his 15st 4lb came crashing down for the last time. It was Foreman's twenty-fifth birthday.

The late Wal Bartleman, boxing writer for the *Evening Standard*, arrived late the following day for Foreman's Press conference beside the pool at Kingston's Sheraton Hotel. Wal jumped out of a taxi, dashed into the dark foyer of the hotel, was shown where to go for the Press conference, shoved open the double doors that led to the pool, came out into the blinding Caribbean sun, took three faltering steps and fell headlong into the pool. Wal was well into his sixties at the time, but took it like a good 'un. 'Never thought after all these years I'd take a dive,' said Wal as he boarded the flight home, still dripping.

This period of the 1970s was a Golden Age of heavyweight boxing: a triumvirate of Ali, Frazier and Foreman, any one of whom might have beaten the others. Just off-stage were Jimmy Ellis, Jerry Quarry, Oscar Bonavena, Earnie Shavers, Cleveland Williams and Ken Norton. There was Joe Bugner and, just before him, Henry Cooper.

I first saw Henry box when he was a seventeen-year-old amateur with the Eltham (Kent) club. He and his twin brother George were so alike I used a mnemonic to identify them. George had a gap in his front teeth, so I said: 'G for Gap, G for George'. I wish I could have found an equally useful guide to the Bedser twins, whom I could never sort out, and still can't.

The Kray twins were easier. One was always chubbier than the other. How come I knew the Krays? I watched them box, amateur and pro, in their young days. Somewhere in the files of *Sporting Record* is a small story on them, in which I naïvely wondered whether they would ever be as famous as the Bedsers. As it happened, they were.

The Cooper twins signed up as professional boxers with manager Jim Wicks on 29 July 1954, in BBC's *Sportsview* programme. Peter Dimmock and I were there to witness the contracts. Henry had won two ABA titles at light-heavyweight in 1952 and '53 and decided to move up to heavy. A hand injury kept him out of the 1954 ABAs and that was the end of his amateur days.

Left *George Foreman hasn't sprouted wings. Those are the arms of the referee signalling the end of Joe Frazier's reign. Foreman beat him inside two rounds in Kingston, Jamaica, 1972. The world now had three great heavyweights in action at the same time: Foreman, Frazier and Ali.*

Round about the same time, Joe Erskine, Brian London and Dick Richardson also turned pro. Britain had more heavyweight talent available than at any other time. If we could have built a big man with Henry's left hook, Joe's skill, Brian's cussedness and Dick's raw determination, we would have had a world champion.

Henry's pro career flourished late. Not until 1959, nearly five years after that signing, did he beat Brian London to become Britain's champion. From this point he outstripped the other three. His authority on the domestic scene was such that he won three Lonsdale Belts outright (the Belt became your personal possession after three successful title fights at the same weight).

In 1986, on the night Frank Bruno fought Tim Witherspoon, Muhammad Ali and Henry Cooper came together again in the same place – Wembley Stadium – where they had fought almost a quarter of a century earlier. No greater respect exists than that shown by old boxing rivals, one for the other.

The twins, Henry and George Cooper, striding out together, in step, naturally. George (right) *fought as Jim Cooper because there was already a George Cooper (no relation) boxing.*

Henry's first Belt was priceless, one of the rare pre-war, pure gold Belts with the names of Harvey, Petersen and Woodcock on it. No man had ever won three Belts and no one will again. Today the Board of Control rations its champions to one only – shame.

By 1971 Henry Cooper had been Britain's top man for twelve years and had long surpassed Bombardier Billy Wells's record as our longest reigning heavyweight champion. On 16 March 1971, just eight days after Frazier had beaten Ali in The Fight, Cooper was challenged by Joe Bugner for all three of his titles: British, European and Empire (as it was still known).

Bugner, a child refugee from Hungary when the Soviet tanks

crushed the uprising of 1956, was a difficult man to judge. On his day he could box and punch and look distinctly competent. He could also be dismally ineffective with no punch and, it seemed, scant fervour for the game. At this point we had better remember that in his fifteenth pro fight in 1969, he beat a man who died four days later.

The Cooper-Bugner fight at Wembley Arena ended in acrimony which has not dissolved to this day. My own part in it contributed to the argument. At the end of fifteen rounds I made Henry a clear winner, but Harry Gibbs, Britain's best referee, held up Bugner's hand. My commentary went thus: 'I find that amazing. How can you take away a man's three titles like that?' In cold print it may not sound too critical, but in the querulous tones used on the night, it was a forthright condemnation of Gibbs's judgment.

The crowd booed long and lustily. Henry took it well at the time.

The most controversial fight I ever covered: Joe Bugner's win over Henry Cooper in 1971. I came down on Henry's side and Joe never forgave me.

Joe Bugner treated me with a studied disdain ever after. It took Harry Gibbs a long time to forgive me. I found out much later that his granddaughter was jeered in school. When I heard that, I was sorry I had come out as vehemently as I did. Perhaps that sounds unprofessional, but I knew Gibbs to be a competent and honest official, and there was room on the night for saying so. In other words, I could still have disagreed with Harry, but at least offered the view that his judgment was to be respected.

In retrospect it was the best thing that could have happened to Henry, although he will not agree. The defeat enabled him to retire on a huge wave of public sympathy. His knockdown of Ali, plus this seeming injustice, combined to cloak Henry Cooper in a national popularity which has never waned. He was almost thirty-seven when he quit boxing. Had he gone on, he might have met with stark, decisive defeat.

Throughout his career Henry was managed by the incomparable Jim Wicks, a former bookmaker whose knowledge of the nefarious ways of the world made him a formidable figure in the cut-and-thrust of boxing management. Jim had interesting friends whom one might meet over lunch in Soho.

Albert Dimes was one of them. Dimes was the chap who had an unlicensed fight in a Soho greengrocer's with Jack Spot. I can't remember whether a gun or knife was involved, but it certainly wasn't conducted under Queensberry rules. Dimes was one of Henry's biggest fans and as Jim always said: 'Albert's OK. His sort only duff up other villains.'

Jim's fruity Cockney voice (he was proud of his background and was always citing Tommy Steele and Max Bygraves as other Bermondsey boys) gave vent to some memorable quotes. Whenever Sonny Liston was mentioned as a possible opponent for Henry, Jim would say: 'No, not 'im. 'E's too ugly for us.' And whenever one of Henry's eyes was cut in combat, Jim would tell us: 'Yerss, we was going along very nicely, until *our* eye got done.'

Jim rightly maintained that once you'd beaten an opponent, there was no point in facing him again. He slipped up once, re-matching Henry with the useful American Zora Folley, with dire results. He didn't make too many errors guiding Henry.

On our frequent outings to the Sidney Arms at Sidcup in his later years he was never more than an arm's length away from a phone, so he could get his money down on the day's races. As an ex-bookie he should have known better.

The greatest heavyweight never to turn pro: Cuba's Teofilio Stevenson. I saw him win gold in Munich, Montreal and Moscow, from 1972 to '80, with destructive punches that never travelled more than nine inches. Angelo Dundee tried to tempt him to the States, but he stayed put in Havana.

John McNicholas, a BBC-TV producer, has an engaging sense of humour which Princess Anne discovered at the Moscow Olympics of 1980. During an official inspection of the BBC set-up, she asked McNicholas what his role was. 'Ma'am,' he said, 'I'm in charge of the escape committee.'

Only John's sense of the bizarre could have got me into a ramshackle bus heading into the African jungle in September 1974. I sat beside a native warrior who was in full tribal regalia: head-dress, straw skirt and little else apart from bells jingling on his wrists and ankles. He was also carrying a spear. Every time we hit a rut, his bells jangled, he thumped the handle of his spear on the bus floor, then nudged me in the ribs and grinned. There were two dozen more like him on the bus.

McNicholas was making the BBC preview for the Foreman-Ali fight in Zaire, the former Belgian Congo. His hired troupe of savages would do a war dance in a jungle clearing, while I fronted the action. They may have been fully paid-up members of Equity for all I knew, but I didn't ask to see the menu for lunch in case I was on it.

McNicholas shot back to Britain once he had the preview in the can and left behind the £600 bill for hiring the bus. When Bob Duncan arrived in Zaire he was held hostage for several days until the money arrived from London.

The fight became known as the Rumble in the Jungle (Bundini again). Why Zaire? Because that country was putting up most of the money. George Foreman would stake his world title against Muhammad Ali in a curious, riotously expensive promotion involving Swiss financiers, an English film company, but principally the government of Zaire under its godlike President, Mobutu Sese Seko Kuku Ngbendu Wa Za Banga. Each night before they retired to bed, the citizens of Zaire gazed upon this gentleman's bespectacled face, topped by a leopard-skin cap, as their parting TV image. The head floated on a sea of fluffy white clouds as if it were the nearest thing to heaven.

The President and his government had invested millions upon millions of their citizens' money in this fight in the firm belief that the appearance of Foreman and Ali in Zaire would set off a tidal wave of tourism. If only President Mobutu Seso Seko etc. had asked me, I could have told him he was wrong – at a fraction of the cost. The fighters alone were splitting 10 million dollars – more than 2 million pounds apiece.

The President invited Ali to use his private, palatial villa on the banks of the River Zaire in the suburbs of Kinshasa. Kinshasa, capital of Zaire, is the only city I know where waiters chase rats across the dining-room floor in a four-star hotel and where cars ignite spontaneously on the streets.

John Blashford-Snell, the military explorer, was planning at this time one of his daredevil expeditions: he aimed to navigate the entire length of the river, once known as the Congo, in a small fleet of motorised rubber dinghies. I had a call from his Press Officer. Could I have a word with Ali and persuade him to send a message of goodwill to the expedition, to generate some useful publicity? I told him if he cared to come with me to the presidential villa, he could talk to Ali himself. We duly presented ourselves in Ali's private quarters.

Ali sprawled in an armchair while the PR man knelt beside him and outlined the expedition. Ali's eyes widened and widened. He was fascinated. Angelo Dundee beckoned me over and whispered: 'Who is this guy talking to Ali?' I explained the Blashford-Snell adventure. Angelo said: 'You mean they're gonna navigate this goddam river out here?' It flowed within yards of the villa gardens. I nodded. 'In little rubber boats?' I nodded. 'Jeez,' said Angelo. 'That explains it.' Explains what? I asked. 'Those guys are crazy,' said Angelo. 'That's why Ali's so interested. He's . . . crazy, too!'

Crazy or not, Muhammad Ali pulled off an astonishing feat against Foreman and became, after Patterson, the second man in history to regain the world heavyweight crown. As he predicted:

If you thought it a shock when Nixon resigned
Just wait 'til I kick George Foreman's behind.

The fight was staged in a rundown soccer stadium on the outskirts of Kinshasa at four o'clock in the morning, because of the time difference between Zaire and the USA. I renewed acquaintance with my African warrior friends who were engaged to stamp their feet and brandish their spears throughout the night.

Ali's win was a masterpiece of psychological invention. Foreman, who had won all forty of his professional fights and was still only twenty-five, was a crushing hitter who liked to come after you. Ali was well into his thirties and hadn't been champion for seven years, while the defeat by Frazier raised doubts about his durability. Anyone who understood boxing strategy knew that Ali's only chance was to run and run for several rounds. He would avoid Foreman's big guns while the champion was fresh and strong, perhaps draw some of his strength, then move in to reap some benefit.

So what did Ali do? Like a crazy man, he walked into Foreman from the off and tried to *fight* him! Or he laid back on the ropes and invited Foreman to belt him about the body. It appeared suicidal. But Ali worked out in his ingenious mind that these were tactics Foreman least expected and certainly hadn't planned for. They would confuse him.

They confused me. I could hardly believe what I was watching. I was convinced Foreman's strength would tell. In the eighth round my words were: 'Ali's getting tired. His arms are coming down.' As I said it, Ali lazily propelled himself off the ropes and flung out a right hand in a wide arc. It cracked against Foreman's jaw, spun him through ninety degrees, pitched him nose first to the floor and left him sprawling on his side, with his head up like a drowning man trying

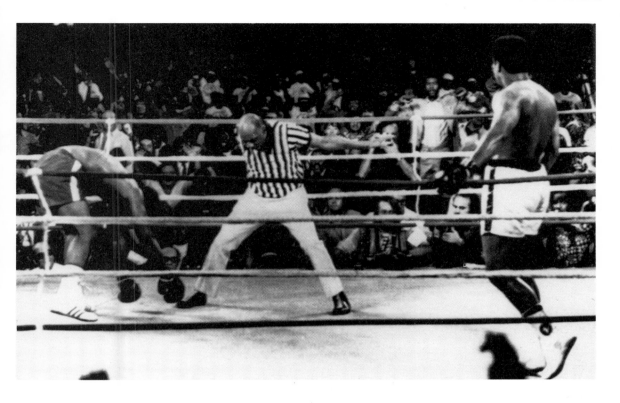

The finest moment of Ali's amazing career. He stuns Foreman into submission in Zaire, 1974, and regains the title. He was thirty-two.

to avoid slipping back through the waves. He was still down there groping for logic in an illogical world when the referee counted ten. I was yelling: 'My God, he's got it back . . . at the age of thirty-two.'

This was the supreme moment of Muhammad Ali's career, far, far better than the two weird fights with Liston. Despite three years' exile and four years pursuing his old title, he was once more The Greatest, leaving Foreman, the man who had lifted Joe Frazier off the floor with one punch, in a crumpled heap. And he'd done it with a strategy no one but himself could have devised.

As my mates the native warriors waved their spears, beat their drums and jangled their bangles in that rickety stadium, rain began to fall. For an hour or more it descended in a massive tropical downpour. Had it started an hour earlier, there would have been no fight. Bob Duncan and I made our way back to Kinshasa along flooded tracks. In the hotel at seven o'clock in the morning, over a Simba beer, he broke the news, with extraordinary gentleness, that my father had died that day in London.

The triumph in Zaire should have been the moment for Ali to retire. I wish he had. The following year in Manila, 'the Thrilla in

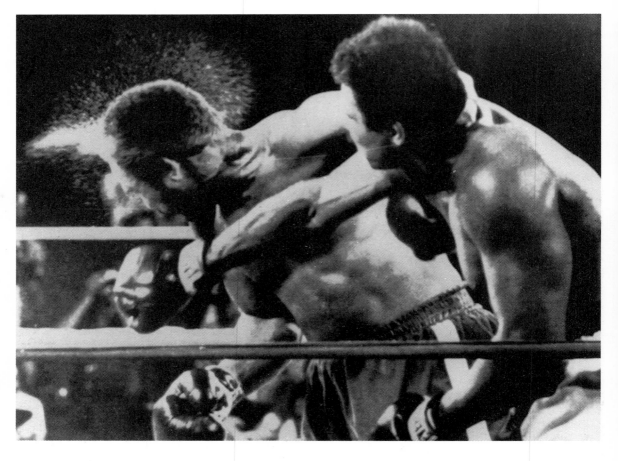

Manila' – Bundini yet again – he and Frazier fought the most gruelling, draining fight I have seen. For fourteen rounds these two great champions stood toe to toe and battered out their third and final meeting. With one round left, Eddie Futch, the wise, compassionate trainer of Frazier, withdrew his man from the fight.

As I climbed through the ropes to interview Ali, I saw him collapse in his corner. This has since been denied. I can only report what I saw. Exhaustion, perhaps the sheer physical relief of not having to face another three minutes with Frazier, overcame him. He still did the interview.

And he still went on fighting. An indication of how little was left came when he lost to the deranged Leon Spinks. His fights no longer had the authentic Ali touch. For whatever reason – I suppose pride, because surely he didn't need the money – he paraded a sad imitation of himself. He professed retirement – and broke his promise.

Third and final clash between Ali and Frazier, the 'Thrilla in Manila', 1975. Frazier was pulled out of the fight after fourteen bitterly fought rounds. Ali should have quit boxing then. Alas, he went on . . . and on.

Right 1978, Ali is thirty-six, and he has just won the heavyweight crown for the third time in revenge against Leon Spinks' earlier victory. Who knows what it was taking out of him?

The most successful heavyweight corner of my time: the little guy in glasses is Angelo Dundee, wizard trainer. Left: *Drew 'Bundini' Brown.* Right: *Walter 'Wali' Youngblood, assistant trainer.*

Left *The fight that should never have happened: Ali's fumbling 1980 challenge to his former sparring partner, Larry Holmes. Ali came out of retirement for this and suffered ten rounds of humiliation and pain. Even this wasn't his final fight. He lost to Trevor Berbick in 1981.*

The final, misguided comeback in 1980 was against the new champion, Larry Holmes, the same Larry Holmes I had watched, year after year, serving Ali as a sparring partner. I am glad I was not at this fight. I sat in the Odeon, Leicester Square, in the small hours, alongside Hurricane Higgins, racked with sadness at the scenes beamed back from Las Vegas.

I can still hear Bundini maniacally urging him on, into more and more terrible punishment, until Holmes was reluctant to throw another punch at his former master, the shambling figure in front of him. It was left to Angelo Dundee to do the only decent thing – get him out of there while he was still alive.

That same year, in London, a young raw amateur was knocking opponents all over the place. I thought he might have quite a future.

The new chap's name was Frank Bruno.

10

The Time Had Come to Relax a Bit

Frank Bruno was a stranger to me in 1980, but I'd read plenty about his big punch and, sure enough, in the ABA build-up that year he won his south-east London title in 40 seconds, his London title in 1min 45sec, and his England title in 52 seconds. He was eighteen years old. I hadn't seen any of these performances, but when he arrived at Belle Vue, Manchester, for his ABA semi-final, he was on TV. His contest with Jim Burns of Rugeley Police petered out tamely in the second round when Burns got a cut eye.

The final at Wembley two weeks later looked sensational on paper, with Bruno matched against Rudi Pika, the Welsh champion, another talented eighteen-year-old. It was an anti-climax. In a messy bout, Bruno convinced two of the three judges he had won. I wasn't so sure and neither was a large section of the crowd.

Frank disappeared from my life for two years. The anticipated conversion to pro boxing didn't happen. Astigmatism in the right eye meant he fell short of British Boxing Board standards. Terry Lawless, who intended to manage Bruno, knew of a surgeon in Colombia who could cut and reshape the muscle that determines the eye's focal length. At Lawless's expense, Bruno set off alone to Bogota to have the operation. He stayed there six weeks, waiting to find out if it had worked. It had. Jose Ignatio Barraquer, the surgeon, told him: 'Everything's fine. You can box again.'

In 1982 Bruno got his British licence. BBC-TV, and I, began

Right *Young Bruno, setting out on his pro career, ten years ago.*

Below *Up-to-date Bruno, with new manager Mickey Duff. They've just heard Frank has got his licence back after an eye operation.*

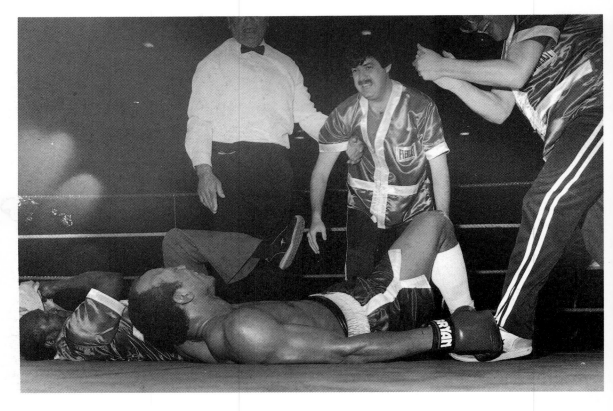

recording the steady sequence of startlingly quick wins which within a year made his name and face familiar to the public.

After seeing his protégé win twenty-one fights in succession (thirteen never got beyond the second round and none of them went the distance), Lawless brought over a 'trial horse' from America, James 'Bonecrusher' Smith, a prison guard and former Army sergeant with a college education. When I asked him why he was known as 'Bonecrusher', he said, 'I've busted some noses and cracked some ribs.' Smith was twenty-nine, seven years older than Frank, but his pro career had not begun until he was twenty-six. He had had fourteen fights and lost just the one – his first.

For nine of the ten rounds Bruno boxed adequately, jabbing away without ever seeming likely to knock Smith out. He was so far ahead when they started the final round he only had to stand up to win. Instead, he got careless, allowed Smith to get through with a stunning left hook, and within seconds a crashing series of blows sent Frank sliding to the floor by the ropes where Harry Gibbs counted him out. Another 74 seconds and the fight would have been over.

If only James 'Bonecrusher' Smith had really been laid flat by Frank Bruno. Smith is actually rolling about in ecstasy, having KO'd Frank in the tenth and final round of their 1984 fight. Frank had it in his pocket, but threw it away.

146

An all-star turnout in Tottenham Court Road. We were celebrating Sportsnight's *500th programme at the Sportsman Club. Seb Coe, Henry Cooper, David Hemery, Ann Packer, Frank Bruno and Bobby Robson are there. So are three* Sportsnight *presenters: David Coleman, Tony Gubba and you-know-who.*

The defeat was so crushing it was another two years before he fought his way back into world title class. It taught him a lesson because when he sits by me at ringside I hear him call out: 'Stay clear, keep your jab going.' He hasn't forgotten Bonecrusher. I'm not surprised.

All those early Bruno fights were seen on *Sportsnight*, the weekly Wednesday programme I inherited in 1975 and fronted, from September to May, for ten years and well over 300 shows, a lot of them under the editorship of Jonathan Martin, who went on to become BBC-TV's Head of Sport. Martin was the genius who decided his frontman should get some first-hand experience of the sports he was introducing.

For years I had commented on the Oxford-Cambridge Boat Race, enjoying the riparian expertise of coaches like H. R. A. 'Jumbo' Edwards and Dan Topolski. Edwards, a soft-spoken former RAF officer, who had rowed in the Race himself in 1926 and 1930, had a mutiny on his hands in 1959 when he was appointed Oxford's coach. The Dark

Blues had lost the last four Races and despondency had set in.

Jumbo, for all his quiet manner, was a martinet with strong views. He introduced Oxford to shovel-shaped oars, which lifted more water from the Thames, but required extreme strength to do so. Oxford won in 1959 and '60. Flushed with success, Jumbo then insisted on extending the outboard length of the oars. I suppose he thought he had supermen in the crew, but they couldn't cope with this Herculean task of leverage. The last time I saw those oars they were on somebody's wall and they were good for a laugh. I don't remember anyone laughing in '61.

Topolski, son of Feliks, the artist who graphically depicted London in the Blitz and later drew the portraits for John Freeman's *Face to Face* programmes, took Oxford to ten successive victories, their longest sequence of wins in more than a century and a half of races against Cambridge. But when he lost the 1986 Race Topolski faced a mutiny, as Jumbo had all those years before. The malcontents were thrown out of the boat and with a crew hastily assembled in the final days before the Race, Oxford won. Fascinating, isn't it, that events

Boat Race Day at Putney. Ronnie Howard (centre), *Oxford Old Blue and race umpire, is trying to organise the toss. I seem to be trying to organise my thoughts.*

What would I have done without her? Phyl and I have been married more than forty years. I suppose in these days of hasty divorce, I should be saying: where did we go wrong?

like the Boat Race, considered staid and traditional, inspire within themselves emotions worthy of soap opera?

Topolski and Colin Moynihan, who coxed Oxford to a seven-lengths win in 1977 and later became Minister for Sport, conspired with Jonathan Martin to put me in the Oxford cox's seat on a practice outing filmed for *Sportsnight*. If you think a cox's job is easy, I can disillusion you. It looks easy, just sitting there twiddling two pieces of rope, but it is intricate and delicate, balancing the power of eight hefty oarsmen pulling the boat through the water at almost 15mph, against the wayward currents of the River Thames. It took me twenty minutes just to steer the boat from mid-river to shore, no more than 100 yards. I'm not sure Topolski's oarsmen were doing their best to help.

Martin also got me into an Olympic racing dinghy as one of Phil Crebbin's crewmen. I spent the best part of a day hanging my bottom out over the Solent, trying to work Crebbin's rotten sails.

I was shoved into a rally car alongside Pentti Arikkola, the Finnish ace. He slung the car round an icy, rutted test track at the Army tank training course, Bagshot. Working hands and feet like a demented organist, Arikkola drove at 70mph, screaming round snow-covered bends within inches of pine trees. It was a virtuoso performance. My commentary? Barely intelligible. How can you speak when you're gibbering with fright?

It was much the same when Jonathan sent me to Brand's Hatch for a morning's entertainment with the late George O'Dell, world champion sidecar driver. I was the passenger. I knelt on a thin sheet of aluminium four inches off the ground and leant out one side or the other to get him round the bends. Try it some time. He touched 180mph going down the straight.

When I arrived at Brand's, I parked alongside an ambulance. I couldn't see its purpose. There was no racing going on. Bob Abrahams, who was filming the sequence, put me wise later. 'I hired it,' he said, 'in case you fell off.'

The *Sportsnight* item which gave me most satisfaction was an interview with Niki Lauda, not long after he was almost burned to death in his car at the Nurburgring in Germany in August 1976. His face and skull were hideously disfigured; one ear virtually disappeared. He was close to death in hospital, a priest was summoned to read the Last Rites. Yet, not many weeks after that accident, this courageous man decided he would race again and I went to Don Mills, Toronto, with Barbara Benedek from the BBC New York office to seek an interview.

We turned up on practice day at 10 am and introduced ourselves to Lauda in the Ferrari pits. He said briefly: 'I have to work. Will you wait?' We waited. Boy, did we wait! At 5 pm he came off the track and said: 'I'm ready.'

We took him to a grassy knoll alongside the track and for an hour or more he spoke of the German ordeal, describing that terrible brush with death in simple, unemotional words. He could even recall the priest's Last Rites. The seven-hour wait (which may have been his way of testing us to see if we were *really* serious) produced the best interview of my life. Later he reproduced it in his book *Formula One* and gave me a painting of himself driving the Ferrari. It hangs proudly on the wall at home.

I started unwinding in the 1980s. I quit *Sportsnight* in 1985, the year I turned sixty. Later I stopped doing greyhound racing and then the Boat Race. Giving up your work is never easy. I enjoyed doing these things, but commonsense tells you it can't go on for ever and the time had come to relax a bit. If it sounds as though everything was

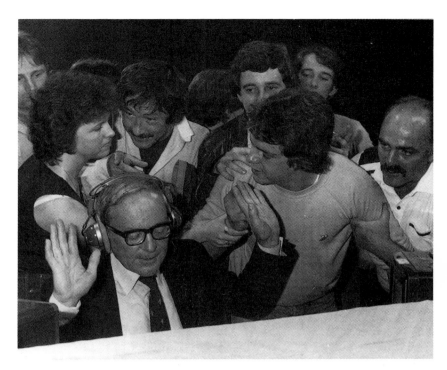

Steady on, chaps, it wasn't my fault . . . Colin Jones of Wales had just been disqualified in Cardiff for hitting an American when he was down.

This is how we worked on the Olympic Games boxing in Los Angeles, 1984. John Shrewsbury (spotted shirt) was the BBC producer who propped me up through two solid weeks of boxing, a mere 342 contests.

coming to an end, I assure you it wasn't – far from it. I didn't plan it this way, but a new relationship – almost a new career – opened up, delightfully. The reason was Frank Bruno.

Frank and Barry McGuigan breathed new life into British boxing. McGuigan created emotional nights in Belfast where the walls of the cavernous King's Hall shook with the ringing cheers he inspired. In the troubled land of Northern Ireland, McGuigan united Catholic and Protestant.

He came to the ring behind a blue flag of peace. His father, Pat, a professional singer, took the microphone and led the willing crowd in 'Danny Boy'. It was breathtaking. The reality, though, was summed up for me one night by a McGuigan fan: 'Sure, while he's fighting, we're behind him as one. But when it's over and we move outside . . .' He didn't have to finish. The message was chillingly clear.

In all the years I have watched, written and talked about boxing, there have been few nights like the one at Queen's Park Rangers football ground in June 1985, when McGuigan challenged the ageing, but still brilliant Eusebio Pedroza of Panama, who had been feather-weight champion of the world for seven years. El Alacran – the Scorpion – had defended his crown nineteen times and hadn't lost a fight of any kind for close on ten years.

B. J. Eastwood, the wealthy Belfast bookmaker who managed Barry, chased Pedroza over thousands of miles and many months before he persuaded him to sign the contract and come to England to defend the title. Pedroza and McGuigan fought fifteen compelling rounds under a summer night's sky until the older man had the title skilfully prised from his hands. Pedroza accepted defeat in front of an ecstatic crowd with grave dignity and was virtually never heard of again.

McGuigan's sublime win roused 25,000 people to a fever pitch of excitement which never swilled over into violence. Men and women danced in the streets of London that unforgettable Saturday night. I had come down from the British Masters golf championship at Woburn and had to return there. As we drove back through Cricklewood the Irish were celebrating McGuigan's great victory on the pavements outside the pubs.

It was reminiscent of nights in Scotland a few years earlier when Jim Watt held the world lightweight title. Watt was a deceptively good boxer, much in the way that other Scottish southpaw, Dick McTaggart, had been. He first impressed himself on me in the 1968 ABA semi-finals in Manchester where he knocked out John Stracey in 45 seconds and went on to win the ABA title at Wembley.

Right *Barry McGuigan, in the arms of Frank Bruno. What must people think?*

Scotsman Jim Watt celebrates a crushing win over John H. Stracey in the amateur championships of 1968. It took Jim another eleven years to become world champion and Glasgow had some great fights.

Left *McGuigan's finest night, brilliantly winning the world featherweight title from Eusebio Pedroza of Panama. Irish pubs in London did record business.*

As a pro he languished for years in Scotland in the shadow of Ken Buchanan, but when he switched camps and joined Terry Lawless in London, his career took off. At the age of thirty, an incredible eleven years after that stunning win over Stracey, he won the world lightweight title, blossoming into a distinguished champion, who defended his title successfully four times. Clean-cut and intelligent, Jim Watt of Glasgow was a credit to his sport and his country. Not a bad TV commentator either.

These last twenty years have been fertile ones for British boxers. John Conteh became our first world light-heavyweight champion since Freddie Mills. John's story mixed success and failure. The success was heady. After four winning world title fights, his future was golden. But it was tarnished when he decided to relinquish the title, on a dubious point of principle, rather than defend it.

Old timers like Jim Wicks would have scoffed at the notion of handing back a world title, the passport to fortune. Conteh never got his title back and for a time his life slid into despair. Fortunately, his wife stood by him and he came out of the spiral with his home intact and his dignity repaired. John has brains and a winning personality. I like to think his best days may still lie ahead of him.

Alan Minter achieved something beyond most British fighters. He went to the USA and won his world title there. Nobody had done that since Ted 'Kid' Lewis in World War I. What's more, Minter took the title from Vito Antuofermo, as durable a middleweight as you could find in those days.

Alan is impetuous and his tongue ran away with him before his fight with Marvin Hagler in 1980. What he said was: 'No black fella is going to take my title.' The National Front soon cottoned on to that. They turned the fight at Wembley into a disgusting racial demonstration.

After two years of lording it over the lightweights, Watt's reign ended at Wembley in 1981, when Alexis Arguello of Nicaragua outpointed him. Jim was almost thirty-three and never fought again.

John Conteh gave British boxing a huge boost with four world title wins at light-heavy between 1974 and '77.

Minter had enough to contend with, without that. Hagler, shaven-headed, menacing and ruthless, quickly cut Minter's face to pieces and hammered him unmercifully. After three rounds, Alan's corner wisely retired him, the signal for an orgy of abuse and bottle-slinging.

One skidded across the ring and caught me a glancing blow on the head while I was still commentating. A little later that night a policeman at ringside told me: 'We've nabbed the fellow who hit you with the bottle.' I asked where he'd found him and he pointed to a place several rows *behind* me. I knew the bottle had come from the

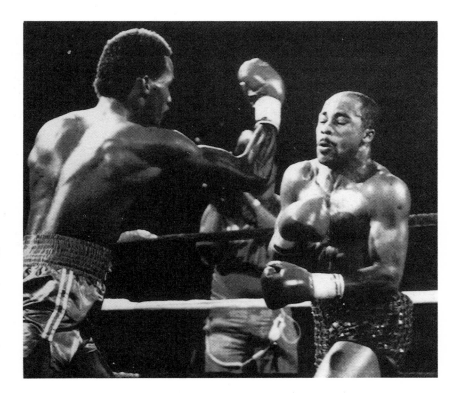

Right *Lloyd Honeyghan* (right) *pulled off arguably the finest British win since Turpin beat Robinson when he slammed Don Curry of America for the undisputed world welterweight title in Atlantic City, 1986. Curry was referred to as 'the best fighter, pound for pound, in the world' – until Lloyd whacked him.*

Top left *A historic moment in Las Vegas, 1980: Alan Minter has just beaten Vito Antuofermo and becomes the first Briton to win a world title in America for over sixty years.*

Left *A regrettable moment at Wembley, 1980: Minter loses the title to Marvin Hagler of America and the crowd start throwing things. I got hit by a bottle.*

opposite direction. A few weeks later I read that a chap had gone down for two months for throwing the bottle that hit me. I expect he's still protesting that he didn't do it. He's right.

Not all that long after Minter, Lloyd Honeyghan went to the States and won his world title there, beating, of all people, Don Curry, recognised at the time as the best fighter, pound for pound, in the world. I said then, and still believe, that this was the finest performance from any British fighter since Turpin's victory over Robinson.

Honeyghan was a late developer. I'd watched him, amateur and pro, for seven or eight years before he came up with this startling win. He was led to the top, slowly and carefully, by Mickey Duff, who regarded him as a pain in the neck.

Lloyd has a mind of his own and doesn't go out of his way to charm anyone. None of that matters when the bell goes. It probably helps. Duff summed it up one day in his matter-of-fact way: 'You don't have to like someone to sign a contract with them.' They made each other a few bob.

*

The hardest part of giving up work came in 1990 when I quit the golf scene. It ended twenty-five years of good times in good company. Peter Alliss was the natural successor to Henry Longhurst. The droll wit, eloquent silence and telling remark exquisitely timed were all reminiscent of Henry. Peter sat on the phrase 'Elementary, my dear Watson,' through four days of the 1977 Open at Turnberry until Watson hit the second to the 18th in the closing moments and shut out Jack Nicklaus.

Alliss cannot contemplate today's mammoth prize money without wincing. In Jacklin's Open at Royal Lytham in 1969, Peter played the best round of the final day, a 66 which elevated him to eighth place. His prize money was £1,100. It was the only time in a long career which included more than twenty victories that he picked up a four-figure cheque. He has made up for it since.

Mark McCormack, the most powerful sports entrepreneur in the world, joined the team each year at the Open. He is the most punctual of men. Time is money, I suppose, and if Mark says he'll be back in the commentary box at 1.35, don't expect him a second earlier or later. His appointments diary is a sheaf of small white cards in his jacket pocket on which he writes with a gold propelling pencil.

Henry Longhurst always eyed him with envy. When Mark left the box to lunch with a client, Henry muttered: 'Off to make another million or two, I suppose.'

What I found astonishing in my time in golf was the turnaround in status between America and Europe. If in 1980 you had dared predict that, within the decade, European golfers would win the US Masters again and again, would take away the Ryder Cup, and relegate American golf to second place, you would have been led away and locked up. It happened, though, and for that we must thank Seve Ballesteros, Sandy Lyle, Bernhard Langer, Nick Faldo and Ian Woosnam.

I fronted golf only once in the States, but it turned out to be the right occasion. In 1987 in Columbus, Ohio, Great Britain and Europe beat the USA 15-13 at Muirfield Village, the course built by Jack Nicklaus on the outskirts of his home town and named after the links where he won his first Open Championship. Shall I ever forget the teasing downhill putt that Eamonn Darcy bravely sank at the 18th on the final day to make certain of victory?

Here was a paramount moment for European golf, the first time the USA had been beaten on their own soil since the Ryder Cup was founded in 1927. It was entirely appropriate that Europe's captain should be Tony Jacklin, the man who lit the fuse under American dominance almost twenty years earlier.

Left Peter Alliss, my golfing chum, in his younger days on the circuit. And he told me he never got in the rough . . .

The boyo himself, affable Eamonn Darcy, after sinking the awkward putt that beat the Americans on their own soil for the first time in the Ryder Cup of 1987.

And yet . . . I felt sorry for Nicklaus, the greatest golfer of all time. That Jack, of all people, should be the first US captain to lose in America, and to lose on his own course in his own town, seemed unnecessarily cruel. It was a further indication of how severely the tide had turned against American golf.

I said goodbye to BBC golf on the Old Course at St Andrews in October 1990, after an Irish victory in the Dunhill Cup. I sat amid a happy crowd on that ancient Roman bridge near the 18th tee and wound up the highlights for the last time. Don't think I wasn't sad. But where better to bow out?

11

'Know What I Mean, Harry?'

I am left with one simple ambition which may never be fulfilled. I want to be ringside, commentating, when a British heavyweight wins the world title. The last to do so was Bob Fitzsimmons, close on a hundred years ago.

Frank Bruno may well have been my last hope. I thought he was going to do it in his 1986 fight with Tim Witherspoon at Wembley, but Frank has never been a relaxed fighter. A little more fluency and less rigid effort would work wonders for him. It was the tiredness from tension that beat him against Witherspoon, despite a vigorous start. After six rounds he was going well. By the end of the seventh, I knew he wouldn't win. Frank's strength was spent.

Witherspoon ended it in the eleventh when Bruno took more punches than he should have done, trapped in a corner, until he fell to his knees. Even then, the referee seemed loath to call it off and Witherspoon bounced some more blows off Bruno's head before Terry Lawless slung the towel in and forced the referee to act.

It was a distressing evening in every way. Frank was badly knocked about and – wrongly – suspected to have a broken jaw. Hooligans attacked the Witherspoon party, hurling chairs at them as they left the ring. The American national anthem was jeered. Police arrested twenty-seven people and had a dozen casualties themselves. Bruno took his defeat with dignity: 'The bruises will heal. Only my pride is hurt. I hope I didn't let anyone down.' But British

Frank Bruno ponders the future. Was he right to carry on boxing? I'm not sure. But he has no doubts and he's the one who has to face the punches.

boxing *had* been let down by its alleged supporters and, as on the night Minter lost to Hagler, I was ashamed of my own countrymen.

Somewhere around this time was born the close affinity between Frank and myself. Our long series of interviews in the ring established his catchphrase 'Know what I mean, Harry?'. Schoolkids started shouting it at me in the street. Then I found relations and friends taking it up.

The BBC had exclusive rights to all his early fights and Frank was accustomed to the little guy in glasses coming at him with the mike when he'd done his work. Fifteen months after the Witherspoon fight he went to the Spurs football ground to take on Joe Bugner. For the first time ITV had a Bruno fight.

He saw Joe off in eight rounds. Into the ring stepped Jim Rosenthal to do the interview. I was sitting at home watching it on the box. I nearly fell out of the armchair when Frank took one look at Jim and uttered the immortal words: 'Where's Harry?' From that moment our relationship was established. *Spitting Image* took us up, and Frank and I, and our families, became firm friends.

Right Wembley, 1986, and for six rounds Bruno does well against world champion Tim Witherspoon, then he starts to tire. Five rounds later, it's all over. Witherspoon remains the champion.

The bond has led us into weird and wonderful events, like making commercials for brown sauce and toilet paper, and doing a double act at the Palladium in the Royal Variety Performance before The Queen. We were handed a two-minute cross-talk script and told the words would be floated up on autocue at the back of the stalls. Frank insisted we memorise every word. So, on the night of the show, we dodged up and down the narrow corridors backstage, shoving past Sir John Mills, Jerry Lewis, Edward Woodward, Tina Turner and Freddie Starr, trying to find a quiet corner where we could rehearse.

'Come on, Harry,' said Frank. 'One more go . . . know what I mean?' He wouldn't let go until we were word perfect.

When the Royal show is over all performers are lined up on the stage to greet The Queen. Frank and I were placed centre-stage, second row, immediately behind The Gauchos, a troupe of bolo-whirling Argentines whose fiery act had been the hit of the evening. Her Majesty moved along the front row from our right until she came to The Gauchos, where she stopped and quietly congratulated them on their act. Then The Queen moved slowly on and had gone no

Don King, US fight promoter, puts his arms round Bruno and Tyson during the build-up to their 1989 fight. Frank and Mike are clearly wondering how much it's going to cost them.

Oh, dear . . . Frank is in trouble already and the fight is barely a minute old. But before this first round is over, he makes Tyson wobble. And a year later, Tyson is no longer champion.

more than a yard away when Frank looked down at me from his 6ft 3in and boomed like a foghorn: 'Harry, she's blown you out!'

We've been to Buckingham Palace together to meet Prince Philip and we've been there separately to receive medals from The Queen. The years with Frank have been very special.

If only he could have whacked Mike Tyson. Well, he *did* whack him, as a matter of fact, but not often enough. Frank's second attempt to lift the heavyweight crown, in Las Vegas, February 1989, came just forty years after the commentary at the factory canteen in Willesden.

Bruno trained longer and harder for this fight than for any other. He could not have been fitter – just as well, because that fitness got him through the first terrible minute when he almost went under to Tyson's ferocious barrage. But, then, near the end of that opening round, Frank threw a right hand which shook Tyson to his heels. When I asked Mike two years later if he recalled the punch he said: 'Remember it? Man, no one's ever hit me as hard, not even Buster Douglas. I blacked out. I'm not kidding.'

I enjoyed working ringside with Mike Tyson. His grasp of boxing history is uncanny.

When Frank landed that punch, objectivity which had carried me through four decades of broadcasting disappeared. I yelled: 'Get in there, Frank!' Very unprofessional. I can only plead that, up there, was my mate Bruno hurting Tyson, my mate Bruno threatening to fulfil that one remaining ambition of mine.

But Tyson, being Tyson, survived and went on to win in the fifth. The Bruno punch, however, made 'Iron Mike' look vulnerable for the first time in his career. The fact was not lost on other fighters. Tyson had been seen to be an ordinary mortal who could be hurt.

One year later in Tokyo, Tyson came unstuck against a journeyman boxer, James 'Buster' Douglas, and unquestionably contributed to his own downfall. Just before Christmas 1989, I went to Las Vegas to present a BBC Sports Review of the Year Award to Tyson. It was clear to me then that he was enjoying the Vegas high life rather than concentrating on the Douglas fight, which was less than eight weeks away. But it was still Frank Bruno who had shown the world that Tyson could be beaten, even if Mike himself had not yet understood it.

Tyson, had we known it, was losing the battle outside the ring as well. Three years to the month after the Bruno fight Tyson stood in an Indianapolis court accused of raping a black beauty contestant, who had accompanied him to his hotel bedroom in the small hours. He was convicted and sentenced to six years in jail. A twelve-year journey, from prison to prison, was over.

In 1980, when Tyson had just turned fourteen, Cus D'Amato, former manager of Floyd Patterson, secured his release from reform school in upstate New York. Cus moulded the delinquent into a world champion, although sadly he died a year before Tyson won the title.

D'Amato also found a wealthy backer for Tyson. Jim Jacobs, a former world handball champion, had cornered the market in old fight films and Tyson spent endless hours in Jacobs' apartment studying these ancient movies. It accounted for his astonishing knowledge of past champions at all weights, something I discovered when he and I sat down in a BBC editing suite at Shepherds Bush and ran through the champions from Jack Johnson onwards.

Tyson had respect for D'Amato and Jacobs, but both men died within a year or two of each other. Tyson was left without a guardian.

I always found that Mike Tyson, treated with courtesy, responded with courtesy. My wife will tell you the same. Here was a man who found too few friends, but plenty of people eager to exploit his money and his fame. Not surprisingly, he responded with equal cynicism. That path led straight back to the cells.

As the '80s turned into the '90s the threads that held my career together were pulled in. Black-tie dinners on the executive floor of Television Centre filled me with nostalgia. We celebrated Peter Dimmock's seventieth birthday. He and I were young men feeling our way in the strange new world of television when we first met. Our paths had crossed ever since.

In 1991 we toasted Paul Fox on his knighthood and wished him well on his retirement as Managing Director of BBC-TV. I had sat alongside Paul on the sub-editor's desk at the *People* in the early 1950s and put innumerable commentaries on fights that went into his *Sportsview* programmes.

Later that year came the retirement of Alan Hart, former Controller, BBC-1, who spent ten years of his life editing the magnificent *Grandstand* which has brightened the nation's Saturday afternoons for well over thirty years.

In the spring of 1991, Brian Barwick, editor of *Sportsnight*, asked me to do an interview with Frank Bruno at Terry Lawless's Royal

Oak gym in Canning Town, where Frank was training. He was known to be contemplating a return to the ring and I thought he might just confirm it in the interview.

I rang him up and asked him what he was going to say. He laughed: 'Harry, be patient. I've got an exclusive for you.' When he said that, I was sure I was right.

I turned up at the gym for the three o'clock appointment one Monday afternoon. Bruno was shadowboxing in the ring. A camera crew stood by. I was saying hello to Frank when someone tapped me on the shoulder. I thought it was a bit rude, to be honest. I looked round and this fellow in a grey tracksuit beamed at me. He had a big red book under his arm. It was Michael Aspel. I had been conned into appearing on *This Is Your Life*. Conned, I may say, not only by Bruno and Barwick, but by my own wife, who knew all about it.

The initial shock takes some getting over, but the rest of that day is unforgettable. My mother, now in her nineties, was in the audience. My daughter-in-law, Bernadette, and her children, Aurélie-Anne and Tim, came over from France. My son, away on business in the Far East, recorded a message. So did Mike Tyson, Arnold Palmer, Virginia Wade and Muhammad Ali. There were

One or two golden oldies on display at this BBC celebration of Peter Dimmocks's seventieth birthday. That's Peter seated at the centre of things. A remarkable man. He virtually founded BBC Television sport and masterminded the 1953 Coronation coverage, which turned TV into the nation's favourite medium. Apart from that, he gave me my first commentary in 1949.

19 February 1991, a very special day. Best bib and tucker on for a trip to Buckingham Palace to receive the OBE from Her Majesty.

personal appearances by Peter Alliss, Henry Cooper, Dan Topolski, Dan Maskell and, of course, Frank.

To cap it all, the men I'd talked and written about down the years came crowding on to the stage. All had won Olympic or world titles: Dick McTaggart, Terry Spinks, Terry Downes, Walter McGowan, Howard Winstone, John H. Stracey, Alan Minter, John Conteh, Chris Finnegan, Charlie Magri and Lloyd Honeyghan.

I was privileged to be there when they had their great moment. Now I was honoured that they had taken the trouble to be there for mine.

One of the men I travelled the world with – we were good friends and rivals – was the late Peter Wilson, boxing writer and sports columnist of the *Daily Mirror*. His son is Julian Wilson, the BBC racing commentator.

Peter (he hated being called Pete, which was what the Americans always insisted on) was known for his hard-hitting, forthright opinions. He had a superior line in literary invective and could expose a charlatan with one vitriolic sentence. The *Mirror* labelled him 'The Man They Cannot Gag'.

He slicked his hair back with a pair of silver-backed brushes, wore a belted camel-hair overcoat with a black Anthony Eden hat, and carried a silver-topped swordstick, in case one of his many victims tried reprisals.

His style might not pass muster in what he would undoubtedly call these 'namby-pamby' days. He once described a cut eye as 'gaping like an unzipped purse', and he didn't mess about finding a simile for the colour of Ezzard Charles's skin. It was, he wrote, 'as black as a yard up a chimney at midnight.'

He was a fine tennis reporter and one of his major triumphs – although it is scarcely remembered today – was a daily television report on the day's happenings at Wimbledon. It went out late at night on BBC-TV in the 1950s and was called *Today on the Centre Court*.

To describe how it was put together is like recalling some obscure event from the Middle Ages. He worked with a film crew and when the main match of the day reached a crisis in a set, he was whistled down from his perch in the Press box, handed a mike, and began commentating.

When the set was won, or the crisis had passed, he returned to the Press box and resumed writing his *Mirror* column. And so it went on, perhaps for several hours: a match that looked like ending in the third set – and had been commentated on accordingly – struggled on into five sets. And still Peter picked up the mike and found the words to fit the new climax.

It was a miracle of journalistic wizardry and expert film editing. Some of these old programmes are in the archives. They remain a tribute to the men who put them together, not least to Peter Wilson.

In the opening to this book I told how Peter Dimmock dragged me from obscurity into the limelight because his commentator had let him down.

The man who couldn't keep his date with Dimmock that night was Peter Wilson.

Index

Page numbers in *italic* refer to photographs

Abrahams, Bob 150
Adams, Bill 67
Ahlquist, Eddie 56
Alexander, John 14
Ali, Muhammad *76*, 83, 86–92,
    86–90, 123–9, *125*, *128–9*, *132*,
    137–43, *139–43*, 170
    see also Clay, Cassius
Alliss, Peter *94*, 100, *160*, 161, 171
Andrews, Eamonn 23–4, *23*, 36–7,
    37, 84
Ankrah, Roy *38*, 39
Arikkola, Pentti 149–50
Armstrong, Henry *13*
Aspel, Michael 170

Baer, Max *13*
Ballesteros, Seve 96
Bartelman, Wal 131
Barwick, Brian 169
Becker, Boris *112*
Benedek, Barbara 150
Benvenuti, Nino 57
Beyfus, Gilbert 50, 51
Blashford, John 137
Bloomfield, Andy 118

Boon, Eric 12, *13*, 25–6, *26*, 83
Borg, Bjorn *110*, 122
Bowman, Bob 12
Boys' World 16, *17*
Brazier, Brian 65–6
Brown, Drew 89, 143, *143*
Brown, Joe 'Old Bones' 59
Bruno, Frank 143–7, *145–7*, 152,
    153, 163–8, *164–7*, 169–70
Buckley, Johnny 34
Bugner, Joe 133–5, *134*, 164
Bundini (Drew Brown) 89, 143, *143*
Burns, Jim 144
Butler, Frank *42*

Caldwell, Jim 65
Cardus, Neville 22
Carnera, Primo *91*
Carpenter, Adelaide *10*, 170
Carpenter, Clive 39, *95*, 170
Carpenter, Harry (Snr) *10*, 12, 13
Carpenter, Phyllis 22–3, *95*, *149*
Cawley, Evonne *116*
Charnley, Dave 57, 59, *59*
Clark, Clive *94*
Clarkson, Bob 100

Clay, Cassius 56–7, *57*, *58*, 69, 71, 75–83, *75–82*, 84–6
  see also Ali, Muhammad
Cockell, Don *13*, 29–30, 43, *44*, 50–1
Coe, Seb *147*
Coleman, David 67, *96*, 108, *147*
Condon, John 127
Connors, Jimmy *109*, 120
Conteh, John 155–6, *157*, 171
Cooper, George 131, *133*
Cooper, Henry 54, 75, *77*, *79*, *80*, 81, 91, 131–3, *132–3*, 134–5, *147*, 171
Coventry, Harry 100
Cowgill, Bryan 67
Cox, Bill 100
Crebbin, Phil 149
Critchley, Bruce *94*
Curry, Don 159, *159*

Daily Mail 39, 40, 46–7, 66
Dalby, W. Barrington 26, 32–3, *35*
Dam, Luc van 29
D'Amato, Cus 169
Danahar, Arthur 12, 26, *26*
Darcy, Eamonn 161, *162*
Davis, Frankie 38
Dempsey, Jack *48*
Dimes, Albert 135
Dimmock, Peter 18–19, 53, 66, 69, 126, 131, 169, 172
Docherty, Sam 49
Donner, Terry 27, *27*
Dosse, Philip 22
Downes, Terry *13*, 60–2, *61*, 171
Duff, Mickey 36, 60, *145*, 159
Duncan, Bob 72–3, *91*, 92, 126, 137, 139
Dundee, Angelo 62, 81, 85, 89, 138, 143, *143*
Durham, Yancey 'Yank' 126
Dyson, Geoff *54*

Edberg, Stefan *113*
Edgar, Barrie 20, 23
Edwards, H.R.A. 'Jumbo' 147–8

Elliott, Herb *64*
Erskine, Joe 54, 132
Evert, Chris *117*

Fagan, Steve *82*
Farr, Tommy 12–13
Finnegan, Chris 72–3, 171
Fisher, Humphrey *35*
Fisher, John 65
Flanagan, Bud *77*
Fleischer, Nat 56, 75, 87
Foreman, George 72, 129, *130*, 131, 137, 138–9, *139*
Fox, Paul 17, 53–4, *54*, 169
Francis, Roy 37–8
Frazier, Joe 71, 126–31, *128–30*, 140, *140*

Gains, Larry 12, *25*
Gallico, Paul 46–7
Gardiner, Gerald 51
Gardner, Jack 50, 52
Gibbons, Bill 16–17
Gibbs, Harry 134–5, 146
Glendenning, Raymond 32–3, *34*
Goddard, Lord Chief Justice 51
Goolagong, Evonne *116*
Graf, Steffi *118*
Grandstand 67, *68*, 169
Gubba, Tony *147*

Hackett, Desmond 41, *42*
Hagler, Marvin 157, *158*
Hart, Alan 169
Hart, Oliver 16
Harvey, Len 12, *13*
Hay, Alex *94*
Hemery, David *147*
Henderson, Eugene 32, 61
Henderson, Michael 9, 11–12, 18, 20
Hoban, Leo 19
Holmes, Larry *142*, 143
Honeyghan, Lloyd 159, *159*, 171
Howard, Ronnie *148*
Huffleman, Mike 100

Ibbotson, Derek *65*

Jacklin, Tony 104–5, *105*, *106*, 107, 161
Jacobs, Jim 169
Johansson, Ingemar 54–6, *55*
Johnson, Ron 20
Jones, Ann 108, *114*
Jones, Doug 75–6

Kearns, Jack 'Doc' 45
Kettley, Les 89, 90–1
King, Billie-Jean 108, *115*
King, Don *166*
King, Freddie 20
Kramer, Jack 118, *120*

La Motta, Jack 31
Lakeland, Ray 93, 99
Lauda, Niki 150
Lawless, Terry 144, 146, 155, 163
Leonard, Sugar Ray 71–2
Lesnevich, Gus *13*, 29
Liston, Charles 'Sonny' 69, *70*, 71, *71*, 83–7, *86*
London, Brian 54, 91, 132
Longhurst, Henry 94, *99*, 103–4, 107, 161
Louis, Joe 69, *72*, 123, *124*
Lu, Mr 96
Lucas, Laddie *96*

Macartney, Clem 16
McCarthy, Sammy *13*, *38*, 39
McCormack, Mark 161
McEnroe, John *111*, 120, 122
McGowran, Bill 49
McGuigan, Barry 152, *153*, *154*
Mackay, Angus 37
McMillan, Roy 64–5
McNicholas, John 136–7
McTaggart, Dick *48*, 49, 57, 65, 171
Madigan, Tony 56, *58*
Mann, Bill 22
Manning, J.L. 49
Marciano, Rocky 43, *44*, *45*, 46
Marshall, Lloyd 29–30
Martin, Jonathan 147, 149, 150
Maskell, Dan 118, 119, *120*, 171

Matthews, Phyl 22–3
Metcalfe, George 39
Middleton, George *33*
Miller, Johnny 96
Mills, Don 150
Mills, Freddie *28*
Minter, Alan 156–7, *158*, 171
Monaghan, Rinty *13*
Moore, Archie 43, 45–6, *45*
Moore, Brian 22
Moynihan, Colin 149

Nastase, Ilie *109*, 119–20
Navratilova, Martina 108, *118*, 122
Nicklaus, Jack 96, *97*, 98, 100, *102*, 103, 161, 162

O'Connor, Terry 49
Odd, Gilbert *48*
O'Dell, George 150
Olympic Games 49–50, 71–3, *151*

Packer, Ann *147*
Palmer, Arnold 100, *101*, 104, 170
Parker, Jack 14, 16
Pastrano, Willie 62
Patterson, Floyd 55, *55*, 56, 69, 71, *71*, 91
Pedroza, Eusebio 152, *154*
Pender, Paul 34, 62
Perry, Cornelius 62, *63*
Petersen, Jack 12, *13*
Phillips, Tom *42*
Pietrzykowski, Zbigniew 56–7, *57*, *58*
Pignon, Laurie 49, 50
Pirie, Gordon *64*
Potgieter, Ewart *28*

Quarry, Jerry 123, *125*

Ratcliffe, Terry 20
Read, Bob 16
Reekie, Pat 41, 43
Richards, Derek 64
Robinson, Sugar Ray 30–2, *31*, *32*, 33–6, *61*, 62, 74–5

Robson, Bobby *147*
Rosenthal, Jim 164
Round, Dorothy 110
Rudkin, Alan 66

Saraudi, Giulio *58*
Saunders, Don 56
Schaap, Dick 74
Scott, Don 20
Seller, Nat 29
Sharpe, Ivan 22
Shrewsbury, John *151*
Smith, James 'Bonecrusher' 146, *146*
Smith, Stan *109*, 119
Solomons, Jack 12, *13*, 24–7, *25*, *28*, 29–30, 36, *42*, 61, 75, *77*, 79
Sommerfield, Teddy 66
Speedway Gazette 14, *15*
Spinks, Leon 140, *141*
Spinks, Terry 49, *51*, 171
Sporting Record 21–2, 39
Sportsnight 147–50
Sportsview 53–4, *54*
Stevenson, Bill 49
Stevenson, Teofilio *136*
Stockton, Dave 98–9
Storey, Basil 14, 16
Stracey, John H. 152, *155*, 171
Stuart, Duggie 40
Sunday Graphic 16, 17

Taylor, Frankie 'Tiger' 65
Tidy, John 118

Tiger, Dick 60, 61
Titchener, Dan 13–14, 18
Topolski, Dan 147, 148–9, 171
Trevino, Lee 105, 107
Turpin, Randolph *13*, 29, 30, *30*, *31*, 32, *32*, *33*
Tyson, Mike *166–8*, 167–9, 170

Van den Burgh, Tony 21

Wade, Virginia 108, *116*, 170
Walcott, Jersey Joe *86*, 87
Walker, Billy 62, 63, 64
Walker, George 64
Walter, Gerald 41, *42*
Wardell, Michael 21
Wareham, Arthur 46
Waterman, Peter *13*
Watson, Tom 96, *97*, 98
Watt, Jim 152, 155, *155*, *156*
Webb, Ellsworth ('Spider') 61
Weill, Al 43, 45
West, Peter 118, *120*
Whiting, George 41
Wicks, Jim 131, 135
Wilkinson, Slim 103
Williams, Johnny *13*
Wilson, Peter 41, *42*, *70*, 171–2
Witherspoon, Tim 163, *165*
Wood, Lainson 22, 29
Woodcock, Bruce *13*, 50
Woodcock, Vic 14

Youngblood, Walter 'Wali' *143*